the Barbecue book

the Barbecue book

Barbara Logan

This edition produced exclusively for

 WHSMITH

Produced specially for W. H. Smith & Sons by
Ward Lock Limited, 82 Gower Street,
London WC1E 6EQ, a Pentos Company.

Text filmset in Rockwell Light
by MS Filmsetting Limited, Frome, Somerset

Printed and bound in Spain by Graficromo, S.A., Cordoba

CONTENTS

Notes

It is important to follow *either* the metric *or* the imperial measures when using the recipes in this book. Do not use a combination of measures.
All recipes serve eight people, unless otherwise specified.

Acknowledgements
The author and publishers would like to thank the following organizations for supplying colour photographs:
British Meat (pages 2–3, page 47); British Sausage Bureau (page 63); Frank Odell Limited (pages 10–11, page 15); New Zealand Lamb Information Bureau (page 19)

Photography on pages 23, 39, 43, 51, 58–59, 67, 87 and 90–91 by Sue Jorgenson
Home Economist Lorna Rhodes
Photography on pages 31, 35 and 75 by Edmund Goldspink

The author and publisher would also like to thank Frank Odell Limited for kindly supplying equipment for photography

INTRODUCTION

The popularity of eating out of doors has brought the barbecue into its own so that it is now accepted as an informal, fun way of cooking as well as entertaining.

It first appeared when man discovered how to kindle a fire and found out that his food tasted better cooked. The next great leap forward in cooking occurred when man invented the spit. The barbecue saw its halcyon days and, indeed, got its name, when it was commonplace for people to celebrate by roasting a whole beast – '*de barbe a queue*' (from beard to tail) on a spit, usually on the village green in Europe or in the cattle- and sheep-grazing prairies and pampas of far-off lands.

Today, barbecuing has become far more sophisticated. Nevertheless, the barbecue itself remains essentially a very simple means of cooking and can easily be improvised almost anywhere.

Perhaps the main reason why barbecuing has become so popular is that all manner of aids and gadgets have been developed to help anyone become a master barbecue chef. One has only to look at the displays of barbecuing equipment and accessories at garden centres and department stores to appreciate how well the barbecuing enthusiast is catered for – from simple braziers to gas and electrically operated models, some of which incorporate ovens, hoods or windshields, to name just a few variations.

CHOOSING A BARBECUE

If you have never used a barbecue before, the best advice is to help at other people's barbecue parties. Some hosts will let their guests cook their own steaks, for instance, and, with a little encouragement, the experienced barbecue chef might be persuaded to pass on some of his secrets, for barbecuing is inclined to be a highly individual art.

Assuming, then, that our beginner has had an initiation into barbecuing without necessarily undergoing a veritable 'trial by fire', he or she should select one of the following basic alternatives:

THE TRADITIONAL HIBACHI
Designed along classical lines and the simplest brazier available, the Hibachi (literally 'fire bowl' in Japanese), consists of a cast iron (or cast aluminium) fire bowl with a removable fire grate, a draught control vent near the base and a cast iron (or aluminium) grill for which there are usually several cooking levels to raise the food above the fire.

While the cooking area of a single Hibachi is small, models are also available with composite table-top units on small wooden bases. Free-standing models are also available on legs and on wheels. All the handles for the grate and for carrying the units are usually made of wood so that the braziers are easily portable. The draught control vent is a great help in lighting the fire, controlling the heat and, later, for removing cinders and ash. Altogether, the Hibachi is simple, efficient and usually inexpensive, and eminently suitable for picnics, caravanning or on the beach.

THE PORTABLE BARBECUE
In its simplest form, this consists of a bowl made of heavy gauge sheet metal to hold the fire and a usually adjustable, revolving wire grill above it. Models vary greatly in shape and size.

The most important points to examine before buying this type of barbecue are the thickness and quality of the metal used for the fire bowl (usually treated with a heat-resistant finish) and of the wire used to make the grill. The fire bowl should be tough enough to stand up to great heat for long periods: additional protection can be given by laying gravel and foil on the fire bowl. The grill should be made of chrome or nickel-plated stout steel wire to withstand the direct heat of the fire below. Additionally, the wires of the grill should be close enough to prevent small pieces of food, such as sausages, from falling through into the fire.

Only braziers with adjustable grills are recommended, so that the grill can be raised through a central pivot or by moving it up or down a set of at least three grill-holders fixed along the circumference of the bowl of the barbecue. Any other way of varying the cooking temperature, such as tilting the grill or revolving it to put the food over a cooler or hotter part of the fire bowl is not entirely satisfactory, except for those usually larger models where the fire-pan itself can be moved up and down.

It should be noted that free-standing barbecues can become rather unstable. In the best designs the legs are usually braced on to a shelf below the barbecue on which food and plates can be stacked. Their combined weight acts as ballast and improves stability.

Extras on many models include a spit rod, kebab holders, windshield, hood, adjustable grill height and undershelf.

WAGON BARBECUES
These barbecues cater for a large number of people. They have generous working areas on either side of the hood and a shelf below on which sturdy legs are braced. Specific features frequently include a spit motor, warming oven, side table, hood and adjustable grill height.

KETTLE GRILLS
These are mostly free-standing, with a hinged hood, and are round or oval in shape. They are made of cast aluminium or steel plate, stainless or enamelled. The hood is capable of standing upright, and in that position also acts as a windshield. The bottom half is the fire bowl and is very deep to accommodate the fire on a grate below the grill. There are adjustable air vents to regulate air flow, temperature and smoked flavour.

The results obtained from cooking on this type of barbecue are very similar to those obtained in an oven except for the effect of the embers and the smoke which the fire makes. The kettle grill is ideal in windy weather, but its greatest virtue

ABOVE *Portable and wagon barbecues*

RIGHT *Two traditional hibachi-style charcoal barbecues*

LEFT Two types of electric barbecues

BELOW Kettle grills

11

must be for the chef who knows exactly how to control the fire and can, therefore, gauge quite accurately when the food is cooked without having to lift the lid too often. It is ideal for the preparation of a single dish, such as a large joint, for a set of persons who will all sit down to the meal at the same time.

ELECTRIC AND GAS OPERATED BARBECUES
These models can be plugged into the electricity mains or into a container of bottled gas which can conveniently be carried on the barbecue. In both cases pieces of volcanic rock take the place of charcoal and briquets. They become red hot and cook in the same way – by radiating heat on to the food on the grill or spit above. The great advantage here is that the barbecue can be set at precisely the degree of heat desired. Neither gas nor electric barbecues produce smoke but this can be obtained by placing chips of dampened hickory or fruit wood on to the heated 'briquets' before closing the hood.

DO-IT-YOURSELF BARBECUES
The barbecue enthusiast can build his own barbecue, having decided beforehand whether or not it is a temporary or permanent structure that is required.

First to the improviser – such as the fisherman who gets a sudden urge to cook his catch. An old bucket makes an ideal barbecue and if it has a hole in the side to serve as an air vent, so much the better. It should be stood on a base of bricks. All the fishermen has then to do is to find something he can use as a grill, such as pieces of wire woven together, bits of expanded metal or, better still, and more easily found, a piece of chicken wire.

If no bucket is available, a few bricks arranged in two rows with something to act as a grill between them will serve the same purpose.

When it comes to searching for fuel, people are best off at the beach where there is usually plenty of driftwood. Elsewhere, they may have to look further afield for firewood, paper, cardboard and dry leaves, all of which can help to kindle the fire.

Building a permanent barbecue by do-it-yourself methods requires sufficient care to ensure that it will not turn out to be a folly, an eye-sore, or a source of discomfort to owner and neighbours alike. There are, of course, ways of avoiding this, especially if a sheltered situation can be found in the garden which fulfils all the desirable, practical and aesthetic considerations. It is safest, however, to have a trial run with a simple temporary barbecue made with a few bricks and a grill. A common secondary stage is a conversion from an existing incinerator; this is not likely to raise problems beyond the actual design so that the resulting installation serves both purposes adequately.

Overleaf are two examples of the sort of barbecue which almost anyone could build or adapt to make their own design. Attachments recommended on page 9 for portable barbecues

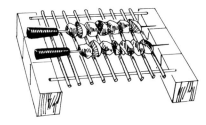

A few bricks and a grid between them is an easy way of creating a simple barbecue

can also be adapted, but however permanent the structure is, these attachments should always be easily removable for storage.

In both cases use firebricks or ordinary bricks.

Method 1
1) Build bricks on three sides to a height of three rows.
2) Use gravel as a base; this aids ventilation.
3) Cover with charcoal.
4) Fit a grill, made either of metal bars, an oven shelf or chicken wire. Gaps between the bars should be narrow so that food cannot fall through.

Method 2 (see right)
1) Build the bricks to a height of four rows.
2) Fit the grid. Metal bars are suitable.
3) Build up another two rows of bricks, incorporating grooves, if liked, to hold a spit or rôtisserie.
4) Fit the grill. Additionally, metal brackets built into the barbecue, with convenient spacing, enable the grill to be moved up and down.

ACCESSORIES FOR THE BARBECUE

Cooking gloves

Apron

Foil – *For the barbecue*: Use, shiny side up, as a protective foundation between the fire bowl and the fire, to make drip trays, to improvise a baking tray, to use as a heat reflector (shiny side downwards).

  – *For the food*: To wrap it up before and during cooking, and to keep it warm once it has cooked.

Sharp knives

Tongs with long handles to stoke the fire and arrange the coals in it, and to handle the food. A pair of shorter tongs are also useful for heavier pieces of meat or fish.

Spatula ⎫
Forks ⎬ each long and with wooden handles
Spoons ⎭

Basting brushes – These should be made of pure bristle; nylon and plastic brushes are inclined to fall prey to the fire.

Stiff metal brush – To keep the grill clean.

Hinged wire baskets – For cooking hamburgers and fish, or for small pieces of chicken or sausages.

Metal skewers (preferably stainless steel) – As long as possible so that the grip does not go over the coals. Wooden handles are recommended.

Spit – This should have three or four pairs of supports on each side of the brazier so that it can be raised, lowered or tilted. It should be suitably thick for its overall length, and have a wooden handle at one end and enough to spare at the other to fit a motor if one is not built in.

  A battery-operated spit motor should have balancing weights to make its task somewhat lighter.

Meat thermometer

Drip pan – For spit roasting. Use either a foil tray or fold a piece of double thickness foil over a piece of wood. Clip the corners together to make the pan leakproof.

Extra forks (or tines) and short or/and four-pronged forks – These can get a better hold of a piece of meat or poultry.

Other Useful Items

Carving board

Large salt and pepper grinders

Sprinkler – small watering can or squirter to douse unwanted flames

Bellows – in case the fire should need a little encouragement

Kitchen roll – indispensible for odd jobs

First-aid kit

A selection of accessories for use on a barbecue

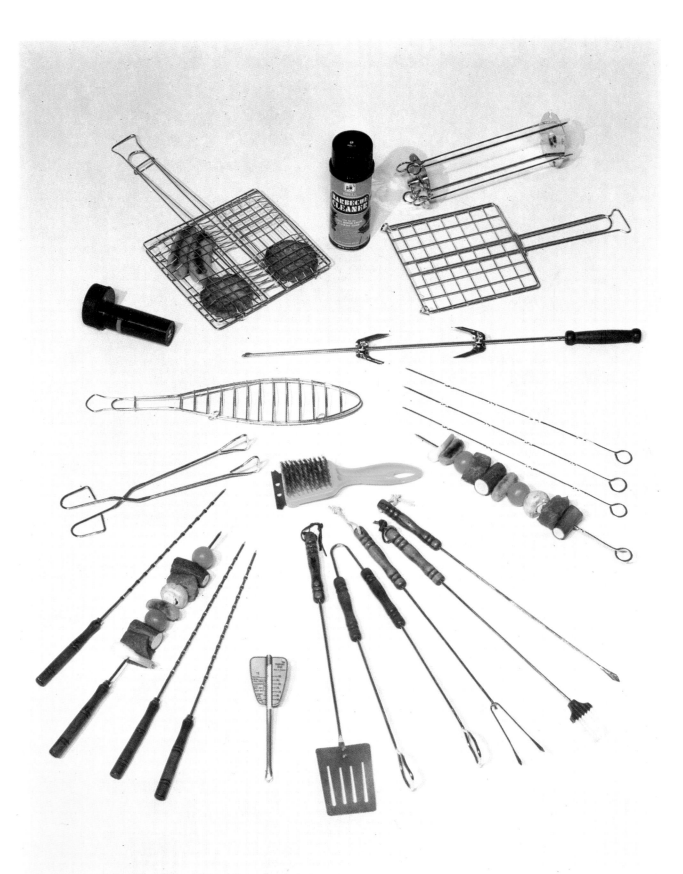

THE FIRE

CHARCOAL

Hardwood charcoal briquets are recommended for good cooking results. They burn longer than lump charcoal and give out more heat. Briquets are uniform in size and so are easier to arrange in the fire bowl. They are obtainable from garden centres, supermarkets, hardware stores and, sometimes, at petrol stations. Light the fire 30–45 minutes before starting to cook.

Specially treated charcoal briquets can be obtained that ignite readily. They do not produce flames and, in fact, unless the draught is very strong, do not glow red in day-time. Instead, a fine grey ash is produced on the surface of each briquet as the fire spreads.

It is particularly important to remember that burning charcoal fumes contain carbon monoxide which is highly poisonous, so that charcoal barbecues should *not* be used indoors.

GAS AND ELECTRICITY

Gas barbecues operate by means of bottled gas, while electric barbecues simply need plugging into an electric point.

FIRE LIGHTERS

Use self-igniting charcoal, lighter fluid or paste, specially treated fire lighters or methylated spirits. There are other liquid fire lighters available but do check what they are made of. Gas torches (or blow-lamps) and electric fire lighters are unquestionably the neatest, cleanest, most efficient and least dangerous.

LIGHTING THE FIRE
There is no reason why anyone should find it difficult to light a
fire if they follow these instructions carefully.

1) Cover the base of the barbecue completely with heavy-duty
   foil or a double thickness of standard foil, shiny side up. If
   you want to lay a fire-base of dry gravel, place another
   sheet of foil over it, but make small perforations in it with a
   fork to allow the air to permeate through to the fire and to
   allow the fat and grease to seep through into the fire-base.
   Leave the coals and cinders above so that they can be
   gathered and conveniently removed after the barbecue is
   over, then sifted from the ash and re-used the next time.
2) Place on the foil whichever you have or prefer of the
   following:
   (a) twisted paper and kindling wood chips
   or
   (b) a few small pieces of specially treated fire lighter and a
   few small pieces of charcoal or broken-up briquets
   or
   (c) small pieces of charcoal and/or briquets and lighter
   fluid or methylated spirits.
3) Put six to eight briquets or larger pieces of charcoal above
   and around whichever you have chosen from 2) and set
   light to it.

Once the fire has caught, it is important to waste no time in
laying on as many more coals as you need, without smothering
it. At this stage, flames can be allowed, but as the fire settles
they will subside. The coals will be at full heat when a thin
layer of grey ash covers them. It is important to aim for a *level*
spread of coals, equally hot, and covering an area preferably a
little larger than the area of the food on the grill above.

Remember also that if the cooking is going to last for some
time, it is important to lay a deeper foundation to the fire and to
have more coals warming on the side ready to add to the
centre. This is because the grill is put completely out of action
as soon as the fire is covered with fresh coals.

For those who like aromatic flavours, add fresh herbs, bay
leaves, sticks of fruit wood, hickory, juniper or a few cloves of
garlic towards the end of the cooking time.

When *spit roasting*, the fire must be stoked rather more
heavily than usual and then split in two by a drip pan in a
furrow down the length of the spit. Alternatively, bank up the
fire along one side of the fire-pan parallel to the spit but a little
away from it, so that the fire-pan can be placed slightly off-
centre in the direction in which the spit is revolving. Light the
fire about 30 to 45 minutes in advance, depending on the type
of fuel used.

SETTING THE SCENE

Safety is all important at any barbecue. Do not wear full sleeves or nylon clothing, keep inflammable substances away from the barbecue area, and never leave children alone by the barbecue or, indeed, near any naked flame.

With this in mind, almost any garden or patio can become a barbecue party area with a little imagination. Large torches and spot lights placed in trees and bushes make good party lights, and fairy lights strung from tree to tree add a touch of magic to the setting. Candles are attractive and give flickering glows but they usually need some protection from the wind. Use candles in bottles in a sheltered spot, but use large dumpy candles or night lights in pottery containers on tables. The sides of the containers will afford some protection. Empty cans, which have a pattern of holes punched all round, also make good sturdy candle holders.

The first thing to greet your guests should be the bar, located away from the entrance and cooking area so as to avoid congestion. An attractive bar can be made with a trestle table, a bamboo pole placed at each corner for uprights, and reed matting, canvas or crêpe paper for a canopy, draped from pole to pole.

Guests often tend to cluster unless you encourage them to move around. The lure of food and drink is a good way to keep people moving, a crisp here, a crudité there, dips and dunks somewhere else. Small tables to hold these tit-bits can be made from empty orange boxes, up-ended and covered with a bright covering. Depending on the amount of room available, spread everything out as much as possible.

Remember that guests at a barbecue usually eat and drink

heartily, so always have plenty of food and drink. The barbecue area should be conveniently close to the kitchen for fetching and carrying and to run an electric extension cord from the kitchen to the spit/rôtisserie motor or an electric barbecue, and for an outdoor spot light. In addition to the cooking area, you will need a side table for the raw food and the aids and accessories required for the barbecuing. These can be covered with foil to keep off insects. Keep any extension cord well marked to avoid accidents.

Have lots of serviettes or kitchen rolls about the place to wipe up sticky fingers etc. A tiered trolley is useful for accompaniments and for stacking used items. Do not forget the coffee pots – these can be kept hot on the side of the barbecue or on small home-made braziers, or the hot coffee can be put into vacuum flasks.

Have plenty of food available at a barbecue – guests always eat heartily

DRINKS, DIPS AND APPETIZERS

A great way to greet your guests is to serve a 'cup' or 'punch' as soon as they arrive so as to get them in the party mood. Wine or beer can be served later on.

Dips, dunks and appetizers are ideal for nibbles. Keep the dunks small and crisp – use carrots, celery or cucumber together with biscuits and crisps. Nuts, olives and gherkins will all help to keep away the pangs of hunger as the delicious smells from the barbecue waft across the garden.

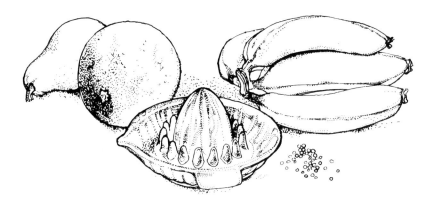

Cider Cup

275g/10 oz canned pineapple
   chunks
150ml/¼ pint dry sherry
finely pared rind and juice of 1
   orange
finely pared rind and juice of 1
   lemon
1.8 litres/3 pints cider, chilled
600ml/1 pint soda water

DECORATION
maraschino cherries
few sprigs mint

Serves 8–12

Mix together the pineapple, its juice and the sherry, orange
and lemon rind and juice, and chill for 1–2 hours. Add the
cider and soda water. Pour into glasses and serve topped with
a cherry and a sprig of mint.

Fruit Juice Cocktail

150ml/¼ pint cold water
150ml/¼ pint fresh **or** bottled lemon
   juice
300ml/½ pint fresh, frozen **or** canned
   orange juice
15ml/1 tablespoon lime juice
100g/4 oz caster sugar
2 egg whites
crushed ice

DECORATION
maraschino cherries

Put all the ingredients, except the cherries, into a cocktail
shaker or screw-topped jar. Cover, and shake well for a few
minutes until light and frothy. Serve in glasses, and decorate
with a cherry on a stick.

Mulled Ale

2 lemons
600ml/1 pint ale
60ml/4 tablespoons brandy
30ml/2 tablespoons rum
30ml/2 tablespoons gin
25g/1 oz Demerara sugar
300ml/½ pint water
2.5ml/½ teaspoon nutmeg
2.5ml/½ teaspoon cinnamon

Serves 6–8

Pare the lemons thinly and squeeze the juice from them. Put all
the ingredients into a pan and heat gently; do not boil. Strain
the liquid and serve at once in punch glasses.

Glühwein

1.2 litres/2 pints red wine
175g/6 oz Demerara sugar
3 sticks cinnamon
2 lemons stuck with 6 cloves
150ml/¼ pint brandy

DECORATION
1 orange, thinly sliced

Put the wine, sugar, cinnamon and lemons into a saucepan. Bring to the boil, then simmer, covered, for 2–3 minutes. Strain the liquid into a jug and add the brandy. Serve the orange slices with the Glühwein.

White Wine Cup

3 oranges
50g/2 oz caster sugar
1 bottle Moselle
ice cubes
1 bottle sparkling Moselle, chilled
225g/8 oz fresh strawberries

Serves 8–12

Slice the oranges very thinly and put into a bowl. Sprinkle with the sugar and add the wine. Cover, and leave the fruit to marinate for 2 hours. Add some ice cubes and the chilled sparkling Moselle. Serve in glasses, decorated with the orange slices and strawberries.

Cream Cheese and Olive Dip

225g/8 oz cream cheese
300ml/½ pint double cream
2.5ml/½ teaspoon curry powder
5ml/1 teaspoon prepared mustard
15ml/1 tablespoon mango chutney
salt and pepper
12 Spanish stuffed olives, halved
milk (optional)

Stir together the cream cheese, cream, curry powder, mustard and chutney until well blended. Add salt and pepper to taste. Stir in the olives, reserving a few for garnish. Add a little milk if necessary to make the correct consistency. Garnish with olives.
Serve with crisps, raw vegetables and biscuits.

Guacamole

2 ripe avocado pears, skinned and
   stoned
1 green pepper, chopped
1 tomato, de-seeded and chopped
25g/1 oz onion, chopped
30ml/2 tablespoons lemon juice
10ml/2 teaspoons olive oil
2.5ml/½ teaspoon ground coriander
salt and pepper

Put the avocado flesh into a basin and mash well with a fork. Add the other ingredients and beat well until smooth. Turn the mixture into a serving bowl, cover and chill for 1 hour before serving.
Serve the Guacamole with blanched cauliflower, celery and carrot sticks, cucumber wedges, crisps or small biscuits.

*Glühwein, Guacamole **and** Party Cheese and Walnut Ball (page 24)*

Piquant Dip

150ml/¼ pint soured cream
45ml/3 tablespoons mayonnaise
few drops Tabasco sauce
5ml/1 teaspoon prepared mustard
10ml/2 teaspoons Worcestershire
   sauce
15ml/1 tablespoon horseradish
   sauce
1 clove of garlic, crushed
30ml/2 tablespoons sherry
salt and pepper

Mix all the ingredients together well. Turn into a small dish and chill well before serving with raw vegetables.

Party Cheese and Walnut Ball

175g/6 oz cream cheese
175g/6 oz strong Cheddar cheese,
   grated
1 green pepper, chopped
1 red pepper, chopped
50g/2 oz spring onions, chopped
4 gherkins, chopped
50g/2 oz raisins
30ml/2 tablespoons sherry
10ml/2 teaspoons Worcestershire
   sauce
100g/4 oz walnuts, chopped

Serves 8–12

Beat together the cream cheese and Cheddar cheese until smooth. Add the other ingredients, except the walnuts, and mix together well. Shape the mixture into a round, wrap in a piece of foil and chill in a refrigerator for 2 hours.
   Put the chopped walnuts in a plastic bag, remove the foil from the cheese ball and put the ball in the bag. Shake well to coat with the nuts. Put the ball in the centre of a plate and surround with biscuits, crisps and crudités.

Kipper Pâté

175g/6 oz frozen kipper fillets
150ml/¼ pint natural yogurt
75g/3 oz gherkins, chopped
good pinch of nutmeg
juice of 1 lemon
salt and pepper

Serves 6–8

Cook the kipper fillets according to the instructions on the packet. Remove any skin and flake the fish into a basin. Add the other ingredients and mix well. Turn the mixture into a small dish and chill well before serving with small biscuits or cheese straws.

Taramasalata

450g/1 lb smoked cod's roe
50g/2 oz onion, finely chopped
1 cooked potato
2 cloves garlic, crushed
50g/2 oz fresh white breadcrumbs
juice of 1 lemon
150ml/¼ pint oil
salt and pepper

GARNISH
black olives, sliced
parsley

Serves 8–12

Put the roe into a basin and beat until smooth. Stir in the onion, potato, garlic and breadcrumbs. Gradually beat in the lemon juice and oil, then season to taste. Turn the mixture into a serving dish, garnish with sliced olives and parsley, and chill before serving with crisps and small biscuits.

VARIATION
The mixture can be piped on to biscuits and decorated with sliced olives.

Olive and Bacon Rolls

8 rashers streaky bacon, rinds
   removed
16 very small button mushrooms
Spanish stuffed green olives

Makes 16

Stretch each bacon rasher and cut in half. Wrap a piece of bacon round each mushroom, spear with a cocktail stick, and grill for about 5 minutes. Place an olive on each cocktail stick, and serve warm.

Spiced Eggs

50g/2 oz butter
2.5ml/½ teaspoon salt
2.5ml/½ teaspoon pepper
2.5ml/½ teaspoon paprika
2.5ml/½ teaspoon cinnamon
8 hard-boiled eggs

Serves 8–12

Melt the butter in a small saucepan, add the salt, pepper, paprika and cinnamon, and cook for 1 minute. Add the eggs and, shaking the saucepan gently, cook until the egg whites turn a light brown.
   Serve the eggs, cut into quarters, with raw onion rings, tomato slices and black olives.

MARINADES, BASTES, SAUCES AND BUTTERS

A marinade is a highly seasoned mixture in which meat and fish can be soaked to tenderize them or to provide a certain flavour before being cooked. Enough should be prepared in which to lay the food so that it can be turned and basted from time to time. If the meat or fish is of a size that makes it difficult to impregnate it with the marinade by turning and basting, then place it in a plastic bag and seal tightly.

In barbecuing, some marinades can also be used for basting and as sauces. Most marinades contain vinegar, wine or citrus juice which acts as a tenderizer, oil or butter to add moisture to very lean meats, and seasonings to add flavour.

A baste is brushed on as the food is cooking and, therefore, does not penetrate in the same way as a marinade. Its main role is to preserve surface moisture, and in certain cases to produce a glazing effect. Basting is particularly important when spit roasting.

When preparing sauces, care should be taken to make sure they blend with the marinades or bastes used on the food before and during cooking. A good stand-by is seasoned butter which can be spread over the food as it melts.

Sweet and Sour Marinade

150ml/¼ pint orange juice
150ml/¼ pint dry white wine
65ml/2½ fl oz white wine vinegar
30ml/2 tablespoons oil
25g/1 oz onion, chopped
15ml/1 tablespoon soy sauce
25g/1 oz Demerara sugar
juice of ½ lemon
2.5ml/½ teaspoon celery salt
ground black pepper

Mix all the ingredients together in a screw-topped jar, cover and shake well. Leave for 1 hour for the flavours to blend, then pour the marinade over prepared chicken, pork or ham and leave for several hours, or overnight in a refrigerator.

White Wine Marinade

150ml/¼ pint oil
300ml/½ pint white wine
salt and ground black pepper
50g/2 oz onion, chopped
1 clove of garlic, crushed
1 bay leaf
25g/1 oz chives, chopped
25g/1 oz parsley, chopped

Mix all the ingredients together in a screw-topped jar, cover and shake well to blend. Pour over fish or chicken and leave to marinate for 2–3 hours.

Lamb Marinade

300ml/½ pint dry red wine
150ml/¼ pint oil
1 clove of garlic, crushed
10ml/2 teaspoons dried rosemary
6 cloves
salt and ground black pepper
15ml/1 tablespoon chopped parsley

Mix all the ingredients together well, pour over the prepared lamb, cover and leave to marinate for 1–2 hours.

VARIATION
Chopped mint can be used in place of rosemary.

Red Wine Marinade

300ml/½ pint oil
300ml/½ pint red wine
2 cloves garlic, crushed
25g/1 oz onion, finely chopped
salt and ground black pepper
1 bay leaf
5ml/1 teaspoon basil
2.5ml/½ teaspoon oregano

Mix all the ingredients together in a screw-topped jar, cover and shake well. Pour over prepared beef and leave to marinate.

Californian Barbecue Baste

150ml/¼ pint oil
150ml/¼ pint red wine
150ml/¼ pint pineapple juice
5ml/1 teaspoon chopped parsley
salt and ground black pepper
2 cloves garlic, crushed

Mix all the ingredients together and use to baste the food during cooking.

Orange and Garlic Baste

300ml/½ pint orange juice
300ml/½ pint oil
60ml/4 tablespoons marmalade
4 cloves garlic, crushed
60ml/4 tablespoons vinegar
20ml/4 teaspoons Worcestershire
   sauce
salt and pepper

Mix together all the ingredients, pour over spare ribs, and leave to marinate for up to 24 hours, then drain and grill.

This mixture can also be brushed on the ribs while cooking them on the grill.

Lemon Barbecue Baste

150ml/¼ pint oil
150ml/¼ pint lemon juice
1 clove of garlic, crushed
2.5ml/½ teaspoon salt
ground black pepper
25g/1 oz onion, finely chopped
2.5ml/½ teaspoon tarragon

Put all the ingredients together in a screw-topped jar, cover and shake well. Leave overnight to blend the flavours.

Delicious as a marinade and baste for chicken pieces and as a baste for a whole chicken on the spit.

Mustard and Honey Baste

100g/4 oz Demerara sugar
15ml/1 tablespoon dry mustard
30ml/2 tablespoons vinegar
30ml/2 tablespoons clear honey
300ml/½ pint pineapple juice

Mix all the ingredients together in a small saucepan, heat to dissolve the sugar, then simmer for 5 minutes.

Use to brush on ham or burgers while cooking.

Barbecue Tomato Sauce

60ml/4 tablespoons wine vinegar
60ml/4 tablespoons water
75ml/5 tablespoons tomato ketchup
25g/1 oz Demerara sugar
15ml/1 tablespoon Worcestershire
    sauce
salt and pepper

Mix all the ingredients together in a small saucepan, bring to the boil and simmer for 10 minutes.

Tipsy Cheese Sauce

100g/4 oz strong
    Cheddar cheese, grated
150ml/¼ pint sherry
5ml/1 teaspoon dry mustard
1 clove of garlic, crushed
salt and ground black pepper

Melt the cheese slowly in a saucepan. Gradually stir in the sherry, then add the other ingredients and heat for a further 2–3 minutes.
    Serve with grilled sausages and steaks.

Hot Barbecue Sauce

30ml/2 tablespoons oil
50g/2 oz onion, chopped
50g/2 oz celery, chopped
1 clove of garlic, crushed
200g/7 oz canned tomatoes
30ml/2 tablespoons concentrated
    tomato pureé
45ml/3 tablespoons vinegar
15ml/1 tablespoon Worcestershire
    sauce
few drops Tabasco sauce
10ml/2 teaspoons chilli powder
150ml/¼ pint stock
salt and ground black pepper
2.5ml/½ teaspoon paprika

Heat the oil in a saucepan, add the onion and celery, and fry gently for 4–5 minutes. Stir in the other ingredients and simmer for 20–25 minutes.
    Use as a baste and a sauce.

Mustard Sauce

10ml/2 teaspoons dry mustard
30ml/2 tablespoons cold water
50g/2 oz butter
50g/2 oz onion, finely chopped
150ml/¼ pint dry white wine
30ml/2 tablespoons brown sauce
15ml/1 tablespoon clear honey
juice of 1 lemon
salt and ground black pepper

Blend the mustard and water together. Put to one side. Melt the butter in a small saucepan, add the chopped onion, and fry for 2–3 minutes. Add the wine and simmer for 4–5 minutes. Stir in the brown sauce, honey and lemon juice, then season to taste. Remove the pan from the heat and stir in the blended mustard.
　　Serve with hot dogs, sausages or frankfurters.

Raisin Sauce

50g/2 oz butter
25g/1 oz flour
300ml/½ pint stock
50g/2 oz seedless raisins
25g/1 oz flaked almonds
1.25ml/¼ teaspoon ground cloves
1.25ml/¼ teaspoon ground cinnamon
　65ml/2½ fl oz sherry
finely grated rind and juice of 1
　lemon

Melt the butter in a pan, add the flour and cook the roux for a few minutes until golden-brown. Gradually stir in the stock, bring to the boil and simmer for 2–3 minutes. Add the other ingredients and simmer for a further 3 minutes.
　　Serve with barbecued ham.

Bitter Orange Sauce

100g/4 oz bitter marmalade
juice of 2 lemons
15ml/1 tablespoon brown sugar
50g/2 oz raisins

Put all the ingredients into a small saucepan and simmer for 5 minutes.
　　Use as a baste for ham during cooking or as a sauce for serving with ham.

Honey and Sherry Sauce

150ml/¼ pint oil
150ml/¼ pint wine vinegar
150ml/¼ pint sherry
60ml/4 tablespoons clear honey
salt and pepper

Mix all the ingredients together well, and pour over the ribs. Leave to marinate for up to 24 hours. The mixture can also be brushed on the ribs during cooking.

Zesty Horseradish Sauce

150ml/¼ pint double cream
juice of 1 lemon
5ml/1 teaspoon horseradish sauce
10ml/2 teaspoons Worcestershire
    sauce
2 spring onions, finely chopped

Mix together all the ingredients and leave to stand for 4 hours before using.
    Serve with steaks or hamburgers and as a topping for jacket potatoes.

Sweet and Sour Sauce

300ml/½ pint light beer
75g/3 oz orange marmalade
45ml/3 tablespoons soy sauce
25g/1 oz Demerara sugar
10ml/2 teaspoons dry mustard
5ml/1 teaspoon ground ginger
2.5ml/½ teaspoon salt
few drops Tabasco sauce

Mix all the ingredients together in a screw-topped jar, cover and shake well until blended.
    Use as a marinade and for basting pork, ham or chicken.

Marinated chicken awaiting barbecuing

Hawaiian Sauce

50g/2 oz Demerara sugar
30ml/2 tablespoons concentrated
    tomato purée
2 cloves garlic, crushed
30ml/2 tablespoons soy sauce
150ml/¼ pint sherry
150ml/¼ pint oil
45ml/3 tablespoons lemon juice
20ml/4 teaspoons Worcestershire
    sauce
60ml/4 tablespoons wine vinegar
550g/1¼ lb canned crushed
    pineapple

Mix all the ingredients together well, and use some to baste ribs after they have cooked for about 10 minutes on the grill. Serve the remainder separately as a sauce or dip.

Piquant Dressing

45ml/3 tablespoons wine vinegar
finely grated rind and juice of 1
    lemon
5ml/1 teaspoon dry mustard
1 clove of garlic, crushed
150ml/¼ pint oil
salt and pepper
5ml/1 teaspoon dried basil

Mix all ingredients together in a screw-topped jar and shake well.
    Serve with salads.

Sour Cream Apple Sauce

300ml/½ pint soured cream
2 hard green eating apples, grated
30ml/2 tablespoons horseradish
    sauce
salt and ground black pepper

Mix all the ingredients together well about 30 minutes before serving.
    Serve with baked potatoes, spare ribs and pork.

Savoury Butters

100g/4 oz butter, softened
5ml/1 teaspoon chilli powder
or
5ml/1 teaspoon curry powder
or
5ml/1 teaspoon oregano
or
5ml/1 teaspoon chopped chives
or
5ml/1 teaspoon chopped parsley
or
5ml/1 teaspoon chopped mint
or
2.5ml/½ teaspoon dill seed
or
5ml/1 teaspoon tarragon

Mix together the butter and one of the herbs or seasonings.

Horseradish Cream Whip

175g/6 oz cream cheese
25g/1 oz sugar
30ml/2 tablespoons horseradish
  cream
juice of ½ lemon
few drops Tabasco sauce
150ml/¼ pint double cream

Beat together the cream cheese and sugar, then add the horseradish cream, lemon juice and Tabasco sauce. Whip the cream until just stiff and fold into the mixture. Chill before serving.

Serve as a topping for steaks, ham or jacket potatoes.

Barbecue Spread

100g/4 oz butter, softened
2.5ml/½ teaspoon dry mustard
5ml/1 teaspoon salt
5ml/1 teaspoon paprika
1 clove of garlic, crushed
15ml/1 tablespoon sugar
finely grated rind and juice of 1
  lemon
50g/2 oz onion, finely chopped
30ml/2 tablespoons Worcestershire
  sauce
15ml/1 tablespoon tomato ketchup
few drops Tabasco sauce
30ml/2 tablespoons vinegar

Gradually beat together all the ingredients. Store in a covered container in a refrigerator.

Use to spread on steaks during grilling and just before serving.

Note Do not use on very fatty meats.

FISH

Most fish and shellfish can be cooked on a barbecue, but especially good are trout, mackerel and herring because of their high fat content. All fish needs to be handled carefully as it can break up very easily. The fish can be wrapped in foil with butter or put into a greased grill basket so that it can be turned over easily. If the fish is cooked without foil, do baste it frequently to keep it moist during cooking. Use either the baste given in the recipe or melted butter to which has been added a little lemon juice.

COOKING CHART FOR GRILLING

				Cooking Time
Food	Cut	Weight/ Size	Fire Heat	Each Side Well-done (mins)
Fish	Cutlet	2.5cm/1 inch	Medium	4–8
	Fillet	1.25cm/½ inch	Medium	4–6
	Whole	350–450g/ 12–16 oz	Medium	10–15
Shellfish	Lobster (halved)	450–675g/ 1–1½ lb	Medium	30–35
	King Prawns		Medium	5–8

Salmon steaks can be cooked directly over the grill, but mackerel is best cooked in a grill basket

Sole Turnovers

8 fillets of sole
salt and pepper
2.5ml/½ teaspoon basil
8 slices processed cheese
100g/4 oz butter, melted
65ml/2½ fl oz white wine

GARNISH
lemon wedges
watercress

Sprinkle the fish with salt, pepper and basil. Place a slice of cheese on each fillet and fold in half. Mix together the butter and wine and brush over the fish. Put the fish in a well-greased wire grill basket, and cook on the grill over hot coals for 6–8 minutes, turning once and basting frequently with the butter. Serve garnished with lemon wedges and watercress.

Shellfish Parcels

450g/1 lb peeled prawns
8 scallops
salt and pepper
100g/4 oz mushrooms, sliced
100g/4 oz onions, chopped
25g/1 oz capers
50g/2 oz butter
300ml/½ pint single cream

GARNISH
fresh parsley, chopped

Put 50g/2 oz prawns and one scallop on a double thickness of buttered foil and sprinkle with salt and pepper. Repeat with the remaining shellfish. Arrange the mushrooms, onions and capers on the shellfish and dot with butter. Pour over the cream. Wrap the foil loosely over the shellfish to make a neat parcel. Cook on the grill over hot coals for 25–30 minutes. Serve the shellfish with the juices poured over them, and sprinkle with chopped parsley.

Peppy Cod Steaks

150ml/¼ pint oil
65ml/2½ fl oz lemon juice
salt and pepper
8 cod steaks

SAUCE
150ml/¼ pint tomato ketchup
15ml/1 tablespoon chilli sauce
45ml/3 tablespoons lemon juice
15ml/1 tablespoon horseradish
   sauce
30ml/2 tablespoons mayonnaise
10ml/2 teaspoons Worcestershire
   sauce
few drops Tabasco sauce
salt and pepper

Mix together the oil, lemon juice and seasoning. Put the fish on to a well-greased barbecue grill or in greased grill baskets. Baste with the mixture and cook over medium coals for 8 minutes. Brush again with the baste, turn the fish, baste again and cook for a further 8–10 minutes.

Mix together the tomato ketchup, chilli sauce, lemon juice, horseradish sauce, mayonnaise, Worcestershire and Tabasco sauces and salt and pepper.

Place the fish on a serving dish and pour over the sauce.

Smoky Mackerel

8 mackerel, gutted
8 sprigs rosemary

MARINADE
150ml/¼ pint wine vinegar
65ml/2½ fl oz oil
65ml/2½ fl oz lemon juice
25g/1 oz brown sugar
salt and pepper
15ml/1 tablespoon Worcestershire
    sauce
2 bay leaves
2.5ml/½ teaspoon paprika

GARNISH
lemon wedges
fresh parsley

Put the fish into a shallow dish. Mix together the marinade ingredients in a small saucepan and bring to the boil. Cool, then pour the mixture over the fish, and leave to marinate for 30 minutes.

Place the fish in a well-greased, hinged grill basket and put a piece of rosemary on top. Cook on the grill over medium coals for 8 minutes, baste with the remaining sauce, turn and cook for a further 8–12 minutes. Serve garnished with lemon wedges and parsley.

VARIATIONS
Red mullet and trout can be cooked in the same way.

Simple Salmon Cutlets

8 salmon steaks
100g/4 oz butter, melted
juice of 2 lemons
salt and pepper
savoury butter (page 33)

GARNISH
lemon wedges

Put the salmon on a well-greased hinged grill basket. Mix together the butter, lemon juice, salt and pepper. Brush the salmon with this baste and cook over hot coals for 10–12 minutes, turning once but basting frequently.

Top each cutlet with savoury butter and garnish with lemon wedges.

Note If a grill basket is not available, wrap each cutlet in greased foil with some of the baste and cook on the barbecue grill for 15–20 minutes, turning once during cooking.

Herbed Herrings

100g/4 oz butter
salt and pepper
5ml/1 teaspoon coriander seeds
2.5ml/½ teaspoon cardamon
finely grated rind and juice of 2
    lemons
300ml/½ pint natural yogurt
8 herrings, de-headed and gutted

GARNISH
chopped lettuce
lemon wedges

Melt the butter in a small saucepan, add the other ingredients apart from the fish, then brush the fish well with this mixture. Place in a flat grill basket and cook on the grill over hot coals for 25–30 minutes, turning and basting frequently. Serve on a bed of chopped lettuce with lemon wedges.

Stuffed Trout

8 trout, gutted
salt and pepper
175g/6 oz crabmeat
50g/2 oz fresh white breadcrumbs
5ml/1 teaspoon basil
50g/2 oz butter, melted

GARNISH
lemon wedges

Sprinkle the inside of the trout with salt and pepper. Mix together the crabmeat, breadcrumbs and basil, and use to fill the cavity. Place each trout on a piece of buttered foil, brush with melted butter and bring the edges of the foil together to make a loose parcel. Place the parcels on the grill over medium coals and cook for 25–30 minutes. Open the parcels carefully, place the trout on a serving dish, pour over the buttery juices and serve with lemon wedges.

Trout with Almonds

8 trout, gutted
100g/4 oz butter
salt and pepper
grated rind and juice of 2 lemons

GARNISH
100g/4 oz toasted flaked almonds
chopped parsley

Put each trout on to a square of buttered foil. Dot with butter and sprinkle with salt, pepper, lemon rind and juice. Bring the ends of the foil together and seal loosely. Place the foil parcels on the grill and cook over hot coals for 25–30 minutes, turning once during cooking. Open the parcels carefully, place the trout on a serving dish, pour over the buttery juices and sprinkle with almonds and chopped parsley.

Corn-husk Cooked Trout

8 trout, gutted
8 corn husks
butter, melted

GARNISH
lemon wedges

Place each trout in a corn husk. Brush the trout with the melted butter and bring the husk round the fish; tie at the silk end. Put the husks on to the grill and cook for 12–15 minutes, turning once during cooking. Remove the husks and serve the trout with lemon wedges.

Barbecued Sprats

900g/2 lb sprats
75g/3 oz flour
oil

GARNISH
lemon wedges
fresh parsley

Toss the sprats in flour and brush with oil. Put them on the well-greased grill of the barbecue or in a greased, hinged, grill basket, and cook over hot coals for 4–6 minutes, turning once and brushing again with oil. Serve garnished with lemon wedges and parsley.

Peppy Cod Steaks (page 36) **and** *Corn-husk Cooked Trout*

MEAT

GENERAL HINTS ON PREPARING MEAT FOR THE BARBECUE

1) Allow the meat to come to room temperature before cooking so that flavours from bastes and sauces will be better absorbed.
2) Trim off excess fat where necessary, then score the remaining fat on steaks, chops and ham to prevent the outer edges from curling during cooking.
3) Rub the barbecue grill well with oil to prevent food from sticking.
4) Prepare marinades, bastes and sauces well in advance.
5) Season the meat with salt and pepper.
6) Turn foods such as hamburgers, steaks, chops and gammon to achieve a lattice pattern from the grill on which they are cooked.
7) Sear both surfaces of the meat quickly to seal in the juices.
8) Do not poke food with a fork as this will cause the juices to run. Always turn with tongs.
9) Do not crowd the grill since this will give an excess of smoke. Allow a 7.5cm/3 inch gap between the charcoal and the grill.
10) Gammon steaks or large flat pieces of meat which are likely to curl during cooking can be kept flat by piercing through the meat horizontally with a skewer.

COOKING CHART FOR GRILLING

Food	Cut	Weight/ Size	Fire Heat	Cooking Time Each Side		
				Rare (mins)	Medium (mins)	Well-done (mins)
Beef	Steak	2.5cm/1 inch	Hot	5–6	7–8	10–15
	Steak	3.75cm/1½ inches	Hot	6–7	9–10	12–15
	Steak	5cm/2 inches	Med/Hot	8–10	15–18	20–25
	Flank (See **Note**)	Whole	Hot	4–5		
	Tenderloin	Whole	Med/Hot	12–15	18–24	
Lamb	Chops	2cm/¾ inch	Medium	4–5	6–7	8–10
	Chops	2.5cm/1 inch	Medium	5–6	7–8	10–12
	Cutlets	1–2cm/½–¾ inch	Medium	4–5	6–7	8–10
	Breast	2.5cm/1 inch	Medium	4–5	6–7	8–10
Pork	Chops	2.5cm/1 inch	Medium			15–18
	Chops	3.75cm/1½ inch	Medium			19–22
	Spare ribs	Whole	Low			35–45
	Spare ribs	2.5cm/1 inch	Medium			10–12
	Belly strips	1.25cm/½ inch	Medium			10–12
Ham	Steak	2.5cm/1 inch	Low/Med			12–18
	Steak	3.75cm/1½ inch	Low/Med			15–22
Veal	Chops	2.5cm/1 inch	Medium			9–12
	Steak	2.5cm/1 inch	Medium			10–12

Note Flank steak should only be served rare for tenderness.

BEEF

Select good quality meat and have the steaks (fillet, rump, porterhouse and sirloin) about 2–2.5cm/¾–1 inch thick. For rare steaks, cook fairly close to the fire. For steaks that are well-done, cook above the coals. If flank steak is to be served, it must only be cooked rare, otherwise it will be tough. Steaks can be marinated to tenderize them; the longer they are left in the marinade the stronger will be the flavour. Alternatively, just rub with a clove of garlic and brush with melted butter before cooking. For a small party, cook a large steak, then slice for serving.

Simple Grilled Steak

8 steaks
salt and pepper
parsley butter (page 33)

GARNISH
watercress

Place the steaks on the grill, sprinkle with salt and pepper, and cook over hot coals for 12–25 minutes, turning once. Place the steaks on a serving dish, top with parsley butter and garnish with watercress.

Roquefort Steak

8 steaks
salt and pepper
225g/8 oz Roquefort cheese
150ml/¼ pint oil
3 cloves garlic, crushed
60ml/4 tablespoons red wine

Season the steaks with salt and pepper and cook on the grill over hot coals for 12–25 minutes, turning once. Mix together the cheese, oil, garlic and wine. A few minutes before the steaks are completely cooked, spread some of the cheese mixture on each one and cook for the remaining time.

Steak aux Champignons

50g/2 oz butter
3 large onions, chopped
225g/8 oz mushrooms, sliced
2 cloves garlic, crushed
salt and pepper
8 porterhouse steaks, 5cm/2 inches
   thick
65ml/2½ fl oz soy sauce
150ml/¼ pint red wine

Melt the butter, add the onions and mushrooms and fry for 3–4 minutes. Add the garlic, salt and pepper and cook for a further 2–3 minutes. Cut a horizontal slit on one side, through the centre of each steak to form a 'pocket'. Do not cut right through the steak. Fill each 'pocket' with the mushroom mixture. Mix together the soy sauce and wine and brush over the steaks. Cook on the grill over hot coals for 12–15 minutes. Turn once and brush with the sauce during cooking.

Steak au Poivre

25g/1 oz black peppercorns
8 steaks
4 large tomatoes
50g/2 oz butter, melted
15ml/1 tablespoon basil
salt
65ml/2½ fl oz brandy

Crush the peppercorns and rub into both sides of the steaks. Leave to stand at room temperature for 30 minutes. Cook on the grill over hot coals for 10–20 minutes, turning once or twice during cooking. Meanwhile, cut the tomatoes in half, brush with the melted butter and sprinkle with basil and salt. Cook on the grill for 5–6 minutes. Place the steaks on a serving dish with half a tomato on each one. Warm the brandy, ignite and spoon over the steaks.

Simple Grilled Steak, Saucy Onions (page 79) **and** *Jacket Potatoes (page 81)*

Flank Steak Teriyaki

1.8kg/4 lb flank steak (See **Note**)
150ml/¼ pint soy sauce
300ml/½ pint red wine
150ml/¼ pint oil
2 cloves garlic, crushed
salt and pepper

GARNISH
savoury butter (page 33)
watercress

Beat the steak well with a steak hammer or rolling-pin. Put the steak into a dish. Mix together the other ingredients and pour over the steak. Marinate in a refrigerator for at least 12 hours, turning once or twice during this time.

Place the steak on the grill and cook over hot coals for 3–5 minutes on each side. Garnish with savoury butter and watercress.

Note Flank steak should only be served rare.

Steak à la Crème

8 steaks

MARINADE
300ml/½ pint soured cream
finely grated rind and juice of 2
    lemons
150ml/¼ pint oil
2 cloves garlic, crushed
30ml/2 tablespoons Worcestershire
    sauce
5ml/1 teaspoon paprika
5ml/1 teaspoon marjoram
salt and pepper

Mix together the marinade ingredients in a screw-topped jar and shake well. Place the steaks in a shallow dish, pour over the mixture and leave to marinate for 3–4 hours.

Place the steaks on the grill and cook over hot coals for 12–15 minutes, turning and basting with the marinade. Sprinkle with ground black pepper before serving.

Steak Provençale

30ml/2 tablespoons oil
225g/8 oz shallots, chopped
450g/1 lb tomatoes, de-seeded and
    chopped
2 cloves garlic, crushed
salt and pepper
5ml/1 teaspoon basil
15ml/1 tablespoon chopped parsley
8 steaks

Heat the oil and fry the shallots for 4–5 minutes until soft. Add the tomatoes to the frying pan with the garlic, salt, pepper and basil. Cook for a further 3–4 minutes, then stir in the parsley. Season the steaks, brush with oil and cook over hot coals for 12–15 minutes, turning once or twice during cooking. Place the steaks on a serving dish and pile the tomato mixture on top.

Beef Tenderloin Vermouth

1.4–1.8kg/3–4 lb beef tenderloin
150ml/¼ pint oil
300ml/½ pint red wine
150ml/¼ pint lemon juice
2 cloves garlic, crushed
2 bay leaves
salt and pepper
30ml/2 tablespoons dry vermouth

Serves 8–12

Place the meat in a strong plastic bag. Mix together the other ingredients, except the vermouth, and pour into the bag. Tie the bag securely and tip to coat the meat with the liquid. Place the bag in a bowl and chill in a refrigerator for 12–24 hours, turning the bag several times.

Drain the meat and cook on the grill over hot coals for 30–50 minutes, turning and basting with the marinade. Place the meat on a board, sprinkle with the vermouth and cut into slices for serving.

LAMB

Loin and chump chops and cutlets are excellent to cook over the coals. Lamb can be cooked medium-rare with a golden-brown crisp exterior and a slightly pink and moist interior. Breast of lamb cut into small strips, marinated to tenderize and to bring out the flavour, makes a delicious inexpensive dish for informal entertaining.

Sweet and Spicy Noisettes

15ml/1 tablespoon clear honey
10ml/2 teaspoons dry mustard
salt and pepper
15ml/1 tablespoon lemon juice
1 clove of garlic, crushed
8 noisettes of lamb, cut from the loin
425g/15 oz canned pineapple rings
50g/2 oz butter
20ml/4 teaspoons chopped mint

Mix together the honey, mustard, salt, pepper, lemon juice and garlic. Spread this mixture over the noisettes and leave to stand for 20 minutes.

Drain the juice from the pineapple. Put 60ml/4 tablespoons pineapple juice and the butter into a small saucepan, heat to melt the butter, then simmer for 5 minutes. Remove from the heat and add the chopped mint. The saucepan should now be put on the side of the grill to keep warm.

Brush the noisettes with the pineapple baste, put them on the grill and cook over medium coals for 30–35 minutes, turning and basting with the pineapple mixture several times. During the last 5 minutes of the cooking time, put the pineapple rings on the grill and heat through. Serve each noisette on one pineapple ring with any remaining pineapple baste poured over it.

Barbecued Chops Oriental

8 lamb chump chops

MARINADE
1 clove of garlic, crushed
150ml/¼ pint soy sauce
150ml/¼ pint water
salt and pepper

Trim the chops and place in a shallow dish. Mix together the marinade ingredients and pour over the chops. Cover and leave in a refrigerator overnight.

Drain the chops, put on the grill and cook over medium coals for 20–25 minutes, turning several times during cooking.

Serve with hot rice.

Chops in a Parcel

4 hard-boiled eggs, chopped
75g/3 oz fresh white breadcrumbs
2 cloves garlic, crushed
salt and pepper
30ml/2 tablespoons chopped
    parsley
75g/3 oz butter, melted
8 lamb loin chops

Mix together the eggs, breadcrumbs, garlic, salt, pepper, chopped parsley and melted butter. Make the chops into a round and cover each one with the mixture. Wrap each chop in a double thickness of foil and put the parcels on the grill. Cook over medium coals for 30–35 minutes. Open the parcels and serve immediately.

Devilled Lamb Chops

8 lamb chump chops
salt and pepper
30ml/2 tablespoons French mustard
225g/8 oz brown sugar

Season the chops with salt and pepper and spread with half the mustard and sugar. Put on the grill, and cook over medium coals for 5–8 minutes. Turn over and spread with more mustard and sugar, then cook for a further 5–8 minutes.

Rosé Lamb Steaks

8 lamb chops, 2.5cm/1 inch thick,
    cut from the leg

MARINADE
150ml/¼ pint oil
150ml/¼ pint lemon juice
150ml/¼ pint rosé wine
2 cloves garlic, crushed
3–4 sprigs rosemary
salt and pepper
30ml/2 tablespoons chopped
    parsley

Place the lamb in a shallow dish. Mix together the marinade ingredients, pour over the meat and leave for 2 hours.

Drain the meat, place on the grill and cook over medium coals for 20–25 minutes, turning and basting frequently.

Lamb cutlets are excellent when cooked over the coals

Lamb Chops Parmesan

8 lamb chump chops
lamb marinade (page 27)
100g//4 oz grated Parmesan cheese
100g/4 oz butter
grated rind and juice of 1 lemon
1 clove of garlic, crushed

Put the chops in a dish and pour over the marinade, then leave for 2–3 hours. Place them on the grill and cook over medium coals for 12–20 minutes, turning and basting once.

Beat together the cheese, butter, lemon rind and juice and the garlic. A few minutes before serving the chops, top with the cheese mixture. Allow the mixture to start melting before serving.

Buttered Lamb Cutlets

8 lamb cutlets
salt and pepper
oil

HERB BUTTER
100g/4 oz butter
45ml/3 tablespoons chopped
    parsley
45ml/3 tablespoons chopped mint
2 cloves garlic, crushed

Season the cutlets with salt and pepper and brush with a little oil. Put them on the grill and cook over medium coals for 12–18 minutes, turning once and brushing with a little more oil.

Meanwhile, mix together the butter, parsley, mint and garlic. Shape into a roll, wrap in foil and chill in a refrigerator until required.

Serve each cutlet topped with a round of chilled herb butter.

Barbecue Lamb Ribs

1.8 litres/3 pints water
45ml/3 tablespoons vinegar
3 large breasts of lamb, cut into
    riblets

SAUCE
45ml/3 tablespoons soy sauce
45ml/3 tablespoons clear honey
45ml/3 tablespoons plum jam
30ml/2 tablespoons white vinegar
10ml/2 teaspoons Worcestershire
    sauce
10ml/2 teaspoons dry mustard
45ml/3 tablespoons tomato ketchup
juice of 1 lemon

Boil together the water and the vinegar, add the lamb and simmer for 15 minutes.

Mix together the ingredients for the sauce in a small saucepan and heat slowly until blended.

Drain the lamb and arrange on the grill, brush with the sauce and cook over medium coals for 12–20 minutes, turning and basting several times. Serve the ribs with any remaining sauce.

Spicy Barbecued Lamb

3–4 large breasts of lamb

MARINADE
300ml/½ pint cider
60ml/4 tablespoons Worcestershire
 sauce
50g/2 oz Demerara sugar
60ml/4 tablespoons red wine
 vinegar
50g/2 oz onion, finely chopped
5ml/1 teaspoon dried rosemary
salt and pepper

Cut the lamb into strips between the bones with a sharp knife, and place in a dish. Mix together the marinade ingredients in a small saucepan and bring to the boil. Simmer for 3–4 minutes, then leave to cool.

Pour the cold marinade over the lamb and leave for at least 3 hours, turning the meat occasionally. Drain the lamb, put on the grill, and cook over medium coals for 12–16 minutes, turning and basting frequently until crisp and golden-brown.

Serve with lemon wedges.

Butterfly Lamb

1.8–2.25kg/4–5 lb leg of lamb,
 boned and split lengthways (see
 Note)

MARINADE
1 clove of garlic, crushed
salt and pepper
5ml/1 teaspoon chopped mint
50g/2 oz onion, chopped
150ml/¼ pint oil
150ml/¼ pint lemon juice

Make the marinade first. Mix together the ingredients, then put the lamb in a shallow dish, and pour over the marinade. Cover and leave for 4–5 hours, turning occasionally. Drain and reserve the liquid. Place two long skewers through the lamb at right angles to form an X to keep the lamb flat during cooking, or place the lamb in a hinged grill basket. Cook on the grill over medium coals for 1½–2 hours, turning and basting frequently. When cooked, place the lamb on a board and slice thinly.

Note The lamb should be split lengthways so that it lays flat.

PORK

Chump, loin and spare rib chops, belly slices and spare ribs are all good cuts to cook on the barbecue. Pork cut from the leg or fillet is excellent meat to use in skewer cooking. Trim off excess fat before cooking. Pork should always be well cooked.

Barbecued Spare Ribs

Serve at least 350g/12 oz per person. The ribs can be cut into portions, marinated before cooking on the grill and the marinade used as a baste during cooking; this will impart a good flavour as well as giving the ribs a glaze. They will take about 35 minutes to cook if cut into two rib portions but up to $1\frac{1}{2}$ hours if the spare rib is left whole. The ribs can be pre-cooked by roasting in the oven or by covering with spiced water and cooking in a saucepan. Recipes on pages 27–32 can be used for cooking with spare ribs.

To Roast Spare Ribs Before Cooking on the Grill

Put the spare ribs in a shallow dish, pour over a marinade (page 27), cover and leave for up to 24 hours. Drain and put them in a roasting tin; cook at 180°C/350°F/Gas 4 for about 1 hour. When ready to barbecue, put the ribs on to a well-greased grill, brush with the reserved marinade and cook for 10–15 minutes, turning and basting frequently, until glazed and crisp.

To Simmer Spare Ribs Before Cooking on the Grill

(2.75kg/6 lb)
Put the ribs into a saucepan and cover with cold water. Add salt and pepper, a few cloves, 2 bay leaves and 2 cloves garlic. Bring to the boil, then simmer for 30 minutes. Drain well and leave in a refrigerator until required. They can then be cooked on the grill for about 10–15 minutes, basting with a sauce.

To Cook Spare Ribs Straight on the Grill

Cut into two rib portions, rub with salt, put on the grill and cook over medium coals for about 10 minutes, turning once. Start basting with the sauce and continue for a further 25–30 minutes, turning very frequently.

*Barbecued Spare Ribs, Spiced Chicken Kebabs (page 72) awaiting barbecuing **and** Orange and Garlic Baste (page 28) **and** Hawaiian Sauce (page 32)*

Spiced Lemon Chops

8 spare rib pork chops

MARINADE
150ml/¼ pint oil
45ml/3 tablespoons lemon juice
5ml/1 teaspoon nutmeg
5ml/1 teaspoon sage
15ml/1 tablespoon brown sugar

Put the chops into a shallow dish. Mix together the marinade ingredients and pour over the chops. Leave for 2–3 hours.

Drain the chops, put on the grill and cook over medium coals for 25–30 minutes, turning and basting with the mixture several times during cooking.

Cream Pork Fillet

150ml/¼ pint soy sauce
65ml/2½ fl oz dry sherry
5ml/1 teaspoon prepared mustard
salt and pepper
900g/2 lb pork fillet
50g/2 oz butter
350g/12 oz mushrooms
150ml/¼ pint soured cream
1.25ml/¼ teaspoon dill weed
salt and pepper

GARNISH
paprika
fresh parsley, chopped

Mix together in a basin the soy sauce, sherry, mustard, salt and pepper. Cut the fillets in half lengthways, and flatten with a hammer or rolling-pin. Brush with the sherry mixture, put the meat on the grill and cook over medium coals for 15–20 minutes, turning and basting frequently.

Meanwhile, melt the butter, add the mushrooms and fry for 5–6 minutes. Stir in the soured cream, dill weed and salt and pepper to taste.

Cut the pork into slices, arrange on a serving dish and pour the sauce down the centre. Sprinkle with paprika and chopped parsley.

Stuffed Pork Steaks

225g/8 oz chicken livers
50g/2 oz butter
75g/3 oz shallots, chopped
100g/4 oz mushrooms, chopped
25g/1 oz fresh white breadcrumbs
2.5ml/½ teaspoon dill weed
salt and pepper
8 pork steaks
30ml/2 tablespoons oil

GARNISH
chopped parsley

Chop the livers. Melt the butter in a frying pan, add the shallots and livers and fry for 2–3 minutes. Add the mushrooms to the pan and cook for a further 4–5 minutes. Stir in the breadcrumbs, dill weed and seasoning to taste. Cut a pocket in each steak and fill with the mixture. Brush the steaks with a little oil, put on the grill and cook over medium coals for 20–30 minutes, turning and brushing with more oil several times during cooking. Serve sprinkled with chopped parsley.

Cranberry Barbecued Chops

8 pork chops
salt and pepper
175g/6 oz cranberry sauce
60ml/4 tablespoons clear honey
2.5ml/½ teaspoon ground cloves
2.5ml/½ teaspoon nutmeg

GARNISH
chopped parsley

Score the fat on the chops and sprinkle with salt and pepper. Mix together the other ingredients and brush over the chops. Put on the grill and cook over medium coals for 25–30 minutes, turning and basting with the sauce. Arrange the chops on a serving dish, pour over any remaining sauce and sprinkle with chopped parsley.

Gammon Steaks With Seville Sauce

8 gammon steaks
30ml/2 tablespoons oil
60ml/4 tablespoons Worcestershire
  sauce
  grated rind and juice of 2
  oranges
salt and pepper
15ml/1 tablespoon cornflour
300ml/½ pint water
175g/6 oz chunky marmalade

Score the fat on the gammon to prevent curling during cooking, then put into a shallow dish. Mix together the oil, Worcestershire sauce, rind and juice of the oranges, salt and pepper, and pour the mixture over the gammon. Leave to marinate for 2 hours, turning occasionally.

Remove the gammon, reserving the marinade, and cook on the grill over medium coals for 20–30 minutes, turning once and brushing with the marinade.

Meanwhile, put the cornflour in a small saucepan, blend in the water, add any remaining marinade and the marmalade. Bring to the boil, stirring all the time, and simmer for 2–3 minutes.

Arrange the gammon on a serving dish and pour the sauce over it.

POULTRY

Small chickens and ducklings can be cut down the backbone and opened out for cooking on the grill; chicken, duck and turkey portions of varying sizes are also excellent for barbecuing.

Marinate poultry well before cooking, and baste well with a marinade or baste during cooking.

Always cook poultry first with the cut or bony side down towards the coals; the bone helps to act as a heat conductor. If no marinade is used, brush well with melted butter during cooking.

Ducks tend to be fatter than other poultry so their skin should be pricked well with a fork before barbecuing to release the fat; place the drip pan beneath the duck to catch the drippings.

COOKING CHART FOR GRILLING

				Cooking Time Each Side		
Food	Cut	Weight/ Size	Fire Heat	Rare (mins)	Medium (mins)	Well- done (mins)
Poultry	Chicken	Portion	Medium			20–35
	Turkey	Portion	Med/Low			40–45
	Duck and Duckling	Portion	Medium	7–9	10–11	20–30

Paprika Barbecued Chicken

8 chicken portions

MARINADE
300ml/½ pint oil
3 cloves garlic, crushed
100g/4 oz onion, chopped
salt and pepper
90ml/6 tablespoons paprika

Put the chicken portions into a shallow dish. Mix together the marinade ingredients and pour over the chicken. Leave for 3–4 hours, turning the chicken several times.

Drain the chicken, place on the grill and cook over hot coals for 30–35 minutes, turning frequently and basting with the marinade.

Ranch Style Chicken

8 chicken portions
50g/2 oz butter, melted

MARINADE
150ml/¼ pint apple juice
45ml/3 tablespoons oil
10ml/2 teaspoons Worcestershire
    sauce
25g/1 oz onion, chopped
1 clove of garlic, crushed
salt and pepper
5ml/1 teaspoon paprika
10ml/2 teaspoons tomato paste
few drops Tabasco sauce
2.5ml/½ teaspoon dry mustard

Make the marinade first. Put the ingredients into a screw-topped jar, cover and shake well. Put the chicken in a dish, pour over the mixture and marinate in a refrigerator for 12 hours, turning the chicken twice during this time.

Drain the chicken, brush with the melted butter, put on the grill and cook over hot coals for 30–35 minutes, turning and basting with melted butter several times during cooking.

Barbecued Chicken Drumsticks

8 chicken drumsticks

SAUCE
50g/2 oz butter
50g/2 oz onion, chopped
200g/7 oz canned tomatoes
30ml/2 tablespoons Worcestershire
    sauce
25g/1 oz Demerara sugar
salt and pepper

Make the sauce first. Melt the butter in a saucepan, add the onion and fry for 2–3 minutes. Add the tomatoes, Worcestershire sauce, sugar and seasoning, and simmer for 10 minutes. Rub through a sieve or liquidize.

Brush the drumsticks with the sauce, place on the grill and cook over hot coals for 20–25 minutes, turning and basting several times during cooking. Serve the remaining sauce separately.

Lemon Grilled Chicken

4 young chickens, about 900g/2 lb
  each
2 lemons
75g/3 oz butter, melted
salt and ground black pepper
paprika

Split the chickens in half lengthways. Cut the lemons in half and use to rub all sides of the chicken, squeezing the juice over the flesh. Place the chicken in a dish, cover and chill for 3 hours.

Brush the chicken with the melted butter, sprinkle with salt and pepper and place on the grill. Cook over hot coals for 25–30 minutes, turning and brushing several times with melted butter during cooking. Test the chicken with a skewer to see if it is cooked (the juices should run clear).

Crispy Chicken Pieces

100g/4 oz plain flour
salt and pepper
8 large chicken breasts
225g/8 oz butter, melted

Mix together in a plastic bag the flour, salt and pepper. Dip the chicken breasts into melted butter, then put them, one at a time, in the bag and coat thoroughly with the flour. Put the chicken on the grill and cook over hot coals for 8–10 minutes on each side, turning once and basting well during cooking with the melted butter.

Eastern Ginger Chicken

8 chicken portions

MARINADE
150ml/¼ pint oil
150ml/¼ pint white vinegar
15ml/1 tablespoon wine vinegar
1 clove of garlic, crushed
100g/4 oz onion, chopped
15ml/1 tablespoon French mustard
5ml/1 teaspoon ground ginger
30ml/2 tablespoons soy sauce
10ml/2 teaspoons chilli sauce
juice of 2 lemons

Put the chicken portions in a shallow dish. Mix together the marinade ingredients and pour over the chicken. Cover and marinate in a refrigerator for 4–6 hours, turning the chicken several times.

Place the chicken on the grill and cook over hot coals for 30–40 minutes, basting with the marinade and turning several times during cooking.

Golden Crisp Duck

8 duck portions
100g/4 oz dried breadcrumbs
salt and pepper
grated rind of 1 orange
2 eggs
65ml/2½ fl oz orange juice

GARNISH
watercress
orange wedges

Remove the skin from the duck, wash and dry well. In a plastic bag, mix together the crumbs, salt, pepper and orange rind. In a dish, beat together the eggs and orange juice. Coat the duck with the egg mixture, then put the portions, one at a time, in the bag and coat well with the crumbs. Remove the portions from the bag and shake well to remove surplus crumbs.

Put the duck on the grill and cook over medium coals for 35–40 minutes, turning occasionally, until cooked and golden-brown. Garnish with watercress and orange wedges.

Californian Barbecued Chicken

juice of 2 lemons
100g/4 oz butter, melted
salt and ground black pepper
8 chicken portions
Californian barbecue baste (page 28)

Mix together the lemon juice, melted butter, salt and pepper. Brush the chicken with this baste and cook on the grill over medium coals for 35–40 minutes. Turn the chicken while cooking, and brush frequently with the Californian Barbecue Baste.

Mandarin Chicken Bundles

8 chicken portions
salt and pepper
275g/10 oz canned mandarin oranges
3 carrots, cut into julienne strips
juice of 2 lemons
8 sprigs rosemary
15ml/1 tablespoon cornflour
300ml/½ pint chicken stock
chopped parsley

Season the chicken portions with salt and pepper and place each on a square of double thickness foil. Drain the juice from the mandarin oranges, and reserve the juice and a few segments for the sauce. Divide the remaining fruit and the carrot sticks between the chicken. Sprinkle with the lemon juice and add a sprig of rosemary to each piece of chicken. Gather the foil up to make a bundle and put in the coals to cook for 35–40 minutes.

Meanwhile, make the sauce. Put the cornflour in a small saucepan, blend in the stock and reserved mandarin juice, bring to the boil, stirring all the time, and simmer for 2–3 minutes. Add the reserved fruit and the chopped parsley.

To serve, open the bundles, glaze the chicken with a little sauce and serve the rest separately.

*Golden Crisp Duck **and** Californian Barbecued Chicken*

Spicy Spanish Chicken

8 chicken portions

SAUCE
225g/8 oz butter, melted
2 cloves garlic, crushed
salt and pepper
10ml/2 teaspoons paprika
2.5ml/½ teaspoon ground cinnamon
2.5ml/½ teaspoon crushed tarragon

Put the ingredients for the sauce in a small saucepan and heat for a few minutes. Brush the chicken with the sauce and cook on the grill over hot coals for 30–35 minutes, turning occasionally and basting frequently.
  Serve with Savoury Rice (page 83).

Sesame Chicken Breasts

8 chicken breasts

MARINADE
salt and pepper
150ml/¼ pint soy sauce
150ml/¼ pint dry sherry
150ml/¼ pint oil
2.5ml/½ teaspoon ground ginger

GARNISH
25g/1 oz toasted sesame seeds

Put the chicken into a shallow dish. Mix together the marinade ingredients, and pour over the chicken. Leave to marinate for 1–2 hours.
  Drain the chicken and cook on the grill over hot coals for 25–30 minutes, turning and basting with the marinade during cooking. Sprinkle with the sesame seeds before serving.

Mixed Herb Turkey

8 turkey drumsticks

MARINADE
300ml/½ pint sherry
150ml/¼ pint oil
50g/2 oz onion, chopped
15ml/1 tablespoon Worcestershire
  sauce
juice of 1 lemon
1 clove of garlic, crushed
5ml/1 teaspoon thyme
5ml/1 teaspoon oregano
5ml/1 teaspoon rosemary
5ml/1 teaspoon marjoram
salt and pepper

Make the marinade first. Mix together the ingredients in a screw-topped jar and shake well. Leave for 4 hours so that the flavours blend.
  Put the turkey in a dish, pour over the mixture and leave to marinate for 2 hours.
  Drain the turkey, place on the grill and cook over medium coals for 1–1¼ hours, turning and basting with the marinade several times during cooking.

SAUSAGES, HAMBURGERS AND KEBABS

Sausages are great fun to cook on a barbecue, especially where guests cook their own food. Cook either on wetted sticks over the coals, on the grill or wrapped in foil and cooked directly in the coals.

Do not prick sausages before cooking and never prod them during cooking. Blanching them first is an ideal way to seal in the flavour and goodness. Just put them in boiling water and simmer gently for 4 minutes, then drain on kitchen paper and use as required.

Sausages can be threaded lengthways on to skewers for easy handling and to prevent chipolata sausages from slipping through the grill. Diagonal cuts can be made in them to prevent them curling up during cooking. They should be brushed with oil and turned frequently during cooking. To avoid burning, baste with a sauce at the 'turning stage' rather than at the initial cooking stage.

Hot-dogs and frankfurters are already cooked, so that they only need a short time to heat through and obtain the barbecue flavour.

Hamburgers should not be too fatty as this could cause a flare-up on the coals. Serve in warm buns with onions, tomatoes and a variety of relishes.

Kebabs are the most versatile and inexpensive method of barbecuing and are ideal for do-it-yourself parties. Your guests can help themselves to the combination of foods that they enjoy most. Skewers should have wooden handles, be as long as possible and flat rather than round, so that the food does not slip when turned. If preparing the kebabs in advance, try to assemble them with foods that take about the same length of time to cook. Remember to baste the food well and to turn it frequently during cooking.

COOKING CHART FOR GRILLING

Food	Cut	Weight/Size	Fire	Cooking Time Each Side		
				Rare (mins)	Medium (mins)	Well-done (mins)
Sausages		Large	Med/Hot			7–8
		Chipo-lata	Med/Hot			4–6
Hamburgers	(beef)	2.5cm/1 inch	Med/Hot	4–5	6–7	7–10
	(lamb)	2.5cm/1 inch	Medium	5–6	7–8	8–12
Kebabs	(beef)		Hot	4–5	6–8	10–12
(see **Note**)	(lamb)		Medium	6–7	7–8	9–10
	(pork)		Medium			12–18
	(veal)		Medium			12–15
	(fish)		Medium			8–12
	(chicken)		Medium			10–12

Note The kebabs need to be turned frequently during cooking. Use lamb cut from the leg or shoulder.

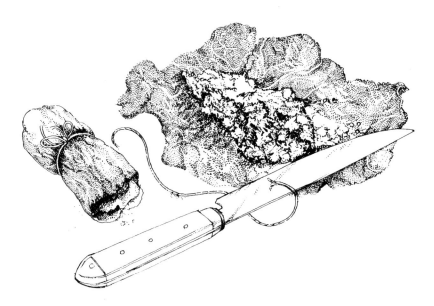

Barbecued Sausages with Sweet and Sour Sauce (page 64)

Barbecued Sausages with Sweet and Sour Sauce

900g/2 lb chipolata sausages
16 small onions

Thread the sausages on long skewers with the onions in between them. Cook on the grill over hot coals, turning frequently, for 12–15 minutes.

Serve with corn-on-the-cob, crusty bread and Sweet and Sour Sauce (page 31).

Turkish Sausages

900g/2 lb chipolata sausages

MARINADE
600ml/1 pint natural yogurt
grated rind and juice of 1 lemon
salt and pepper
50g/2 oz onion, chopped
5ml/1 teaspoon ground ginger
10ml/2 teaspoons curry powder
30ml/2 tablespoons chopped mint

Put the sausages into a shallow dish. Mix together the marinade ingredients and pour over the sausages. Cover and leave to marinate in a refrigerator for 12 hours.

Remove the sausages from the marinade and cook on the grill over hot coals for 10–12 minutes, turning frequently.

Heat the marinade, and serve as a sauce with the sausages. Serve with cucumber salad, mango chutney, toasted nuts and desiccated coconut.

Sausage in a Blanket

8 large sausages
chutney
8 rashers streaky bacon, rinds
    removed

Cook the sausages on the grill over hot coals for 7–8 minutes, turning frequently. Make a cut the length of the sausage, open out and fill with chutney. Wrap a bacon rasher round each sausage, then return to the grill and cook for a further 7–8 minutes, turning frequently during cooking.

VARIATION
Use cheese wedges instead of chutney.

Piquant Sausages

450g/1 lb chipolata sausages
French mustard

ACCOMPANIMENTS
16 long soft rolls
lettuce

Make three diagonal slits in each sausage and spread the mustard over the sausage. Cook on the grill over hot coals for 8–12 minutes, turning frequently during cooking.

Meanwhile, wrap the rolls in foil and heat in the coals. Split them and arrange the lettuce and sausages in each one.

Barbecued Sausages

450g/1 lb sausages

SAUCE
50g/2 oz butter
100g/4 oz onions, chopped
225g/8 oz canned tomatoes
30ml/2 tablespoons tomato ketchup
30ml/2 tablespoons vinegar
30ml/2 tablespoons Demerara
 sugar
10ml/2 teaspoons dry mustard
30ml/2 tablespoons Worcestershire
 sauce

GARNISH
chopped parsley

Make the sauce first. Melt the butter in a frying pan, add the onions and fry for 3–4 minutes. Add the other ingredients and simmer on the grill over medium coals for 15–20 minutes.

Meanwhile, cook the sausages on the grill over medium coals for 12–16 minutes, turning frequently during cooking.

Serve the sausages on a bed of cooked rice with the sauce poured over them. Sprinkle with chopped parsley.

Savoury Herb Patties

450g/1 lb sausage-meat
10ml/2 teaspoons basil
100g/4 oz bacon, chopped
1 onion, grated
salt and pepper
pinch of dry mustard
2 egg yolks
25g/1 oz butter, melted

ACCOMPANIMENTS
8 buns
sliced onion rings
sliced tomato

Mix all the ingredients together, except the butter, and shape into eight small patties. Brush with the melted butter, and cook on the grill over medium coals for 10–12 minutes, turning and basting with butter several times during cooking.

Split the buns and toast them on the grill. Serve each patty in a bun topped with onion rings and tomato slices.

Hot-Dogs Hawaiian

45ml/3 tablespoons oil
100g/4 oz onion, chopped
30ml/2 tablespoons cornflour
10ml/2 teaspoons curry powder
5ml/1 teaspoon salt
275g/10 oz canned crushed
 pineapple
30ml/2 tablespoons vinegar
16 hot-dogs

Heat the oil in a frying pan, add the onion and fry for 4–5 minutes. Mix together the cornflour, curry powder and salt, and stir into the onion. Add the pineapple and vinegar, and cook over low coals, stirring all the time, until the mixture thickens, then simmer for 2–3 minutes.

Put the hot-dogs on the grill of the barbecue and heat over hot coals for 5 minutes, then arrange them on a serving dish and pour the sauce over them.

Tuna Burgers

400g/14 oz canned tuna fish
2 onions, finely chopped
100g/4 oz celery, chopped
15ml/1 tablespoon capers, chopped
15ml/1 tablespoon chopped parsley
10ml/2 teaspoons Worcestershire
   sauce
50g/2 oz fresh white breadcrumbs
salt and pepper
finely grated rind and juice of 1
   lemon
oil

ACCOMPANIMENTS
8 buns
lettuce
sliced tomatoes

Mash the tuna in a basin, then add the other ingredients, and mix together well. Shape into eight burgers and cook on the greased grill over medium coals for 12–15 minutes, brushing with oil and turning several times during cooking.

Split the buns in half and toast them on the grill. Serve a burger in each bun and fill with lettuce and sliced tomato.

Sausage Burgers

900g/2 lb sausage-meat
30ml/2 tablespoons Worcestershire
   sauce
1 onion, chopped
50g/2 oz fresh white breadcrumbs
1 egg
salt and pepper

ACCOMPANIMENTS
8 soft baps
sliced onion rings
sliced tomatoes

Mix together the sausage-meat, Worcestershire sauce, chopped onion, breadcrumbs, egg and seasoning. Shape into eight flat cakes about 7.5cm/3 inches in diameter. Cook on the grill over medium coals for 12–15 minutes, turning once.

Split the baps and toast them on the grill. Serve a burger on each bap and top with the onion and tomato slices.

Cheesy-topped Burgers

900g/2 lb lamb, cut from the
   shoulder
50g/2 oz onion, chopped
30ml/2 tablespoons tomato ketchup
30ml/2 tablespoons Worcestershire
   sauce
50g/2 oz fresh white breadcrumbs
5ml/1 teaspoon dried mint
salt and pepper
25g/1 oz flour

BLUE CHEESE BUTTER
100g/4 oz butter
100g/4 oz blue cheese

Make the butter first. Cream the butter, crumble the cheese and beat into the butter, then form into a roll. Wrap in foil and chill in a refrigerator until required.

Mince the lamb and add the onion, tomato ketchup, Worcestershire sauce, breadcrumbs, mint and salt and pepper to taste. Shape the mixture into eight burgers and coat with a little flour. Cook on the grill over hot coals for 12–18 minutes, turning once during cooking. Just before serving, put a slice of the chilled butter on to each burger. Serve immediately.

Meat turned on the grill will acquire an attractive lattice pattern

Lamburgers with Pineapple

675g/1½ lb minced lamb
2 carrots, grated
2 onions, finely chopped
1 clove of garlic, crushed
1 green pepper, finely chopped
1 egg
15ml/1 tablespoon chopped parsley
15ml/1 tablespoon brown sauce
salt and pepper
8 pineapple slices

ACCOMPANIMENTS
8 soft baps

Mix together all the ingredients, except the pineapple and baps, and shape into eight flat rounds. Cook over hot coals for 15–18 minutes, turning and brushing with oil during cooking. Just before serving, top each burger with a pineapple slice, and cook for a further 2 minutes.

Toast the baps on the grill, and serve the lamburgers in them.

Surprise Hamburgers

900g/2 lb minced beef
salt and pepper
French mustard
1 large onion, sliced into rings

ACCOMPANIMENTS
8 soft baps
tomato ketchup

Mix together the meat, salt and pepper. Shape into 16 thin burgers about 7.5cm/3 inches in diameter and spread half with mustard. Arrange the onion rings on the mustard. Place a second burger on top and press the edges together well. Cook on the grill over hot coals for 12–15 minutes, turning once during cooking.

Split and toast the baps on the grill, and spread half with ketchup. Put a burger inside each one and serve immediately.

VARIATIONS
Cheese or ham slices can be used in place of the onion rings.

Kebabs with Olives

8 rashers streaky bacon, rinds
    removed
900g/2 lb rump steak
16 small tomatoes
16 button mushrooms
16 Spanish olives
oil

Stretch the bacon rashers with the back of a knife. Cut each in half and roll up. Cut the steak into 2.5cm/1 inch cubes. Thread the bacon rolls and steak on to eight small skewers. Thread the tomatoes and mushrooms with the olives on to another eight skewers. Brush the kebabs with oil and cook on the grill for 12–15 minutes, adding the skewers with the vegetables for the last 8 minutes of the cooking time. The kebabs should be brushed with oil and turned several times during cooking.

Serve on a bed of cooked rice accompanied by Barbecue Tomato Sauce (page 29).

Spicy New Zealand Kebabs

900g/2 lb lamb, cut from the leg **or** shoulder
1 green pepper
1 red pepper
16 button mushrooms
50g/2 oz butter, melted

MARINADE
150ml/¼ pint red wine
15ml/1 tablespoon tomato ketchup
15ml/1 tablespoon wine vinegar
10ml/2 teaspoons Worcestershire sauce
25g/1 oz finely chopped onion
salt and pepper
pinch of Cayenne pepper

Cut the lamb into 2.5cm/1 inch cubes and put into a dish. To make the marinade, mix together the wine, ketchup, vinegar, Worcestershire sauce, onion, salt, pepper and Cayenne pepper. Pour over the lamb, cover and allow to marinate for 12 hours, turning occasionally so that all the meat is covered with the marinade.

Cut the peppers in half, remove the seeds and cut each pepper into eight pieces. Thread the lamb, mushrooms, red and green peppers on to skewers and brush with the melted butter. Cook on the grill over hot coals for 10–12 minutes, turning frequently and basting with the marinade.

Souvlakia

900g/2 lb lamb, cut from the leg

MARINADE
16 large bay leaves
30ml/2 tablespoons oil
juice of 1 lemon
5ml/1 teaspoon oregano
salt and pepper

Cut the lamb into pieces the size of a walnut, then make the marinade. Break each bay leaf into four pieces. Mix together with oil, lemon juice, oregano, salt and pepper. Thread the lamb on to skewers with pieces of bay leaf in between, allowing one skewer per person. Put the skewers into a shallow dish and pour the marinade over them. Leave for 1 hour.

Cook the skewers on the grill over hot coals, for 7–10 minutes, turning frequently.

Serve with lemon wedges and a salad.

Oriental Kabobs

450g/1 lb prepared sweetbreads
5ml/1 teaspoon salt
675g/1½ lb lamb, cut from the leg **or** shoulder
16 button mushrooms
16 very small tomatoes

MARINADE
300ml/½ pint dry white wine
juice of 1 lemon
150ml/¼ pint oil
2 cloves garlic, crushed
5ml/1 teaspoon dried rosemary **or** sprigs fresh rosemary
salt and pepper

Make the marinade first. Mix together the wine, lemon juice, oil, garlic, rosemary, salt and pepper.

Put the sweetbreads and salt into a saucepan, cover with cold water, bring to the boil and simmer for 15 minutes. Drain and refresh under cold water. Cut away as much white membrane as possible, then cut the sweetbreads into 2.5cm/ a inch pieces. Cut the lamb into 2.5cm/1 inch pieces. Put the sweetbreads and lamb into a shallow dish, pour over the wine marinade, and leave for 4 hours.

Arrange the sweetbreads, lamb, mushrooms and tomatoes on skewers. Brush well with the marinade and cook on the grill over hot coals for 12–15 minutes, turning and basting frequently.

Serve with Oregano Butter (page 33).

Seekh Kabobs

900g/2 lb minced raw lamb
50g/2 oz fresh white breadcrumbs
100g/4 oz onion, finely chopped
25g/1 oz flour
10ml/2 teaspoons salt
2 cloves garlic, crushed
5ml/1 teaspoon ground cinnamon
5ml/1 teaspoon ground cloves
2.5ml/½ teaspoon chilli powder
finely grated rind and juice of 1
   lemon
ground black pepper
150ml/¼ pint natural yogurt
chopped parsley

Mix all the ingredients together, except the yogurt and parsley. Turn the mixture on to a well-floured board and knead lightly. Divide into 16 pieces and shape each into a sausage, about 10cm/4 inches long. Thread two kabobs lengthways on to eight skewers and cook over medium coals for 8–10 minutes, turning frequently until the kabobs are cooked and golden-brown.

Serve on a bed of cooked rice, spoon over the yogurt and sprinkle with parsley.

Bacon and Sausage Kebabs

16 large sausages
16 rashers streaky bacon, rinds
   removed
8 rings pineapple
16 small mushrooms
50g/2 oz butter, melted

Twist the sausages and cut each in half. Cut each bacon rasher in half and wrap round the sausage. Cut the pineapple rings into quarters. Arrange the sausage, pineapple and mushrooms alternately on the skewers, brush with the melted butter and grill over hot coals for 8-10 minutes, turning frequently and basting with the butter.

VARIATION
Brush the kebabs with Mustard and Honey Baste (page 28).

Brochette of Pork

900g/2 lb pork tenderloin
8 rashers streaky bacon, rinds
   removed
16 button mushrooms
50g/2 oz butter, melted
fine browned breadcrumbs

GARNISH
chopped parsley
lemon wedges

Cut the pork into 2.5cm/1 inch cubes. Stretch the rashers, cut each into three pieces, and form into rolls. Arrange the meat, bacon rolls and mushrooms on eight skewers, starting and ending each with a mushroom. Brush with melted butter and roll each skewer in the breadcrumbs. Cook on the grill over hot coals for 20–25 minutes, basting with butter and turning frequently. Sprinkle with chopped parsley and serve with lemon wedges.

Hawaiian Kebabs

450g/1 lb gammon
450g/1 lb veal
8 tomatoes
425g/15 oz canned pineapple
   chunks
25g/1 oz soft brown sugar
25g/1 oz butter

Cut the gammon and veal into 2.5cm/1 inch cubes. Cut the tomatoes in half. Drain and reserve the juice from the pineapple. Assemble the skewers with the gammon, veal, tomatoes and pineapple chunks, then put into a shallow dish.

Mix together the sugar, butter and pineapple juice in a small saucepan, heat until the sugar has melted, then pour over the skewers and allow to marinate for 30 minutes.

Cook the kebabs over hot coals for 15 minutes, turning and basting frequently.

Indonesian Saté

900g/2 lb boneless veal, cut from
   the leg **or** shoulder
50g/2 oz butter, melted

SEASONING
15ml/1 tablespoon ground
   coriander
15ml/1 tablespoon salt
2.5ml/½ teaspoon chilli pepper
5ml/1 teaspoon ground ginger
2.5ml/½ teaspoon ground black
   pepper
5ml/1 teaspoon cumin seeds

MARINADE
150ml/¼ pint oil
150ml/¼ pint wine vinegar
juice of 2 lemons
50g/2 oz brown sugar
2 cloves garlic, crushed
2 onions, chopped

Cut the meat into 2.5cm/1 inch cubes. Prepare the seasoning by mixing together the coriander, salt, chilli pepper, ginger, black pepper and cumin seeds. Toss the meat in the seasoning mixture and put into a shallow dish.

Mix together the marinade ingredients, then pour this over the meat and leave to marinate for 1–2 hours.

Divide the meat between eight skewers, brush with melted butter and cook on the grill over hot coals for 10–12 minutes, turning and basting frequently.

Serve with a salad in Pitta Bread (page 94).

Veal and Cheese Kebabs

450g/1 lb escalope of veal
8 rashers streaky bacon, rinds
   removed
225g/8 oz Cheddar Cheese
8 tomatoes
16 button mushrooms
oil

Cut the veal into 2.5cm/1 inch cubes. Stretch each bacon rasher with a knife and cut into three pieces. Cut the cheese into 24 cubes and wrap each in a piece of bacon. Cut the tomatoes in half. Arrange the ingredients on skewers, brush with a little oil, and cook on the grill over hot coals for 12–15 minutes, turning frequently and basting with some more oil during cooking.

Serve with Sour Rice Salad (page 85).

Chicken Brochettes with Prunes

24 stuffed olives
24 prunes, soaked overnight,
    cooked and stoned
16 chicken drumsticks
30ml/2 tablespoons flour
2.5ml/½ teaspoon ground ginger
50g/2 oz butter
4 oranges
Lemon Barbecue Baste (page 28)

Place a stuffed olive in the cavity of each prune and press the prune together. Cut each drumstick in half. Mix together the flour and ginger in a plastic bag. Add the chicken pieces and toss to coat them with the mixture. Melt the butter in a frying pan, add the chicken and cook for 8–10 minutes, turning several times during cooking.

Cut each orange into eight wedges. Arrange the chicken, prunes and oranges on skewers, brush with the baste and cook on the grill over medium coals for 15–25 minutes, turning and basting frequently.

Spiced Chicken Kebabs

4 chicken breasts, skinned and
    boned
425g/15 oz canned peach slices
150ml/¼ pint natural yogurt
2 cloves garlic, crushed
50g/2 oz chopped onion
5ml/1 teaspoon ground ginger
5ml/1 teaspoon chilli powder
15ml/1 tablespoon cumin seeds
5ml/1 teaspoon salt

Cut the chicken into 2.5cm/1 inch cubes, then put them into a shallow dish. Drain the juice from the peaches, and cut each slice in half. Put to one side.

Mix together the peach juice, yogurt, garlic, onion, ground ginger, chilli powder, cumin seeds and salt. Pour over the chicken, cover and leave to marinate overnight.

Thread the chicken and reserved peaches on to skewers and cook on the grill over hot coals for 8–10 minutes, turning frequently during cooking.

Serve the skewers on a bed of cooked rice with a salad.

Maryland Kebabs

6 chicken breasts
8 rashers streaky bacon, rinds
    removed
4 bananas
2 red peppers
16 small onions

MARINADE
50g/2 oz soft brown sugar
30ml/2 tablespoons Worcestershire
    sauce
juice of 2 lemons
salt and pepper

Make the marinade first. Mix together the sugar, Worcestershire sauce, lemon juice, salt and pepper. Cut the chicken into 2.5cm/1 inch pieces, put into a dish and pour the marinade over them. Cover, and leave for 6–8 hours.

Cut the bacon rashers in half. Cut each banana into four pieces, and wrap a piece of bacon round a piece of banana. Cut the peppers into 2.5cm/1 inch pieces. Assemble the skewers with chicken, onions, wrapped bananas and peppers. Brush with marinade and cook on the grill over hot coals for 10–12 minutes, turning frequently and basting with the marinade.

Serve on a bed of cooked rice.

Scallop Kabobs

25 scallops
8 rashers streaky bacon, rinds
    removed
24 button mushrooms

MARINADE
150ml/¼ pint oil
150ml/¼ pint white wine
25g/1 oz chopped onion
2 cloves garlic, crushed
30ml/2 tablespoons chopped
    parsley
salt and pepper

Cut each scallop in half. Put them into a shallow dish. Mix together the marinade ingredients and pour over the scallops. Chill in a refrigerator for 3–4 hours, turning the scallops occasionally.

Cut each bacon rasher in half, stretch with a knife, and form into rolls. Assemble the scallops, bacon and mushrooms on the skewers, brush with the marinade and cook on the grill over hot coals for 8–10 minutes, turning frequently and basting with the marinade.

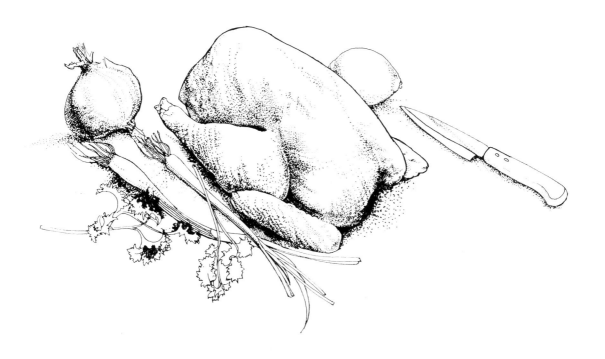

SPIT ROASTING

Spit roasting is one of the delights of barbecuing. Large pieces of meat and poultry cooked in this way are a joy to serve at a party. As the meat turns on the spit, its own juices and any baste used roll round with it so that the meat stays moist and full of flavour. Additionally, the meat will be deliciously crisp and golden-brown when cooked.

Brush the meat generously with a baste or sauce during cooking, and ensure that the drip pan is placed beneath the food in order to catch the drippings.

If more than one piece of meat is to be cooked on the same spit, do not place them too closely together as this will make it difficult for the heat to reach all surfaces. Ensure also that the meat is evenly balanced on the spit otherwise the turning will be jerky and this will result in uneven cooking.

When spit roasting poultry, make the bird as compact as possible with the wings and drumsticks close to the body. Do not put too much stuffing in the bird, as this might then burst out. It is better to put some stuffing in the cavity and use more to make stuffing balls. These can be wrapped in foil and cooked in the coals.

When spit roasting poultry, the birds should be placed on the spit so that the wings and drumsticks are close to the body

COOKING CHART FOR SPIT ROASTING

Food	Cut	Weight	Heat	Cooking Time		
				60°C/ 140°F Rare (hours)	75°C/ 160°F Medium (hours)	95°C/ 190°F Well-done (hours)
Beef	Rolled ribs	2.25–2.7kg/ 5–6 lb	Med/Hot	2–$2\frac{1}{2}$	$2\frac{1}{2}$–$3\frac{1}{2}$	$3\frac{1}{2}$–$4\frac{1}{2}$
	Sirloin	2.25–2.7kg/ 5–6 lb	Med/Hot	$1\frac{1}{2}$–2	$2\frac{1}{4}$–$2\frac{3}{4}$	3–$3\frac{3}{4}$
	Tenderloin	900g–1.35kg/ 2–3 lb	Hot	$\frac{1}{2}$–$\frac{3}{4}$	1–$1\frac{1}{4}$	$1\frac{1}{4}$–$1\frac{3}{4}$
Lamb	Leg	1.8–2.7kg/ 4–6 lb	Medium	$1\frac{1}{4}$–$1\frac{1}{2}$	$1\frac{1}{2}$–2	2–3
	Rolled Shoulder	1.35–2.25kg/ 3–5 lb	Medium	$1\frac{1}{4}$–$1\frac{1}{2}$	$1\frac{1}{2}$–2	2–3
Pork	Loin Boned and rolled	1.8–2.7kg/ 4–6 lb	Medium			$1\frac{3}{4}$–$2\frac{3}{4}$
	Shoulder Boned and rolled	1.35–2.25kg/ 3–5 lb	Medium			$1\frac{3}{4}$–$2\frac{3}{4}$
Poultry	Poussin	350–450g/ 12 oz–1 lb	Medium			$\frac{3}{4}$–1
	Chicken	900–1.8kg/ 2–4 lb	Medium			$1\frac{1}{2}$–$1\frac{3}{4}$
	Duck	1.35–2.25kg/ 3–5 lb	Medium			$1\frac{1}{4}$–2
	Turkey	2.25–2.7kg/ 5–6 lb	Low/Med			2–3

Herb Roasted Turkey

2.25–2.75kg/5–6 lb turkey
salt and pepper
5 shallots, sliced
sprigs parsley
sprigs thyme
75g/3 oz butter

Serves 8–12

Sprinkle the inside of the turkey with salt and pepper. Put the shallots inside the bird with the parsley and thyme. Rub the skin with the butter and sprinkle with salt and pepper. Fasten the turkey on to the spit securely, and cook over low-medium coals for $1\frac{1}{2}$–2 hours.

Honeyed Ducks

2 ducks
salt and pepper
150ml/$\frac{1}{4}$ pint soy sauce
100g/4 oz clear honey

GARNISH
orange segments
watercress

Prick the duck skin all over and sprinkle the inside with salt and pepper. Mix together the soy sauce and honey and rub some into the skin of the ducks. Place the ducks firmly on the spit with either the coals on both sides of the fire bowl with the drip tray in the centre underneath, or with the coals on one side only and the drip tray beneath the ducks. Cook over low–medium coals for $1\frac{1}{4}$–$1\frac{3}{4}$ hours. Brush several times during cooking with the honey baste. For a crisper skin, place the spit nearer to the coals for the last 10 minutes of the cooking time.

Cut the ducks into portions and garnish with orange segments and watercress.

Royal Rib Roast

2–2.9kg/$4\frac{1}{2}$–$6\frac{1}{2}$ lb rib of beef, boned
    and rolled

MARINADE
300ml/$\frac{1}{2}$ pint red wine
30ml/2 tablespoons tomato ketchup
150ml/$\frac{1}{4}$ pint wine vinegar
150ml/$\frac{1}{4}$ pint oil
30ml/2 tablespoons Worcestershire
    sauce
75g/3 oz onion, chopped
salt and ground black pepper
5ml/1 teaspoon rosemary

Serves 8–12

Place the meat in a large plastic bag. Mix together the marinade ingredients, pour into the bag and tie securely. Place the bag in a bowl, then marinate in a refrigerator for 8–12 hours. Turn the bag several times during this period.

Drain the meat, secure it on the spit and cook over medium coals for $1\frac{1}{2}$–$1\frac{3}{4}$ hours, basting occasionally with the marinade.

Remove the meat from the spit, place on a board and slice thinly.

Rosemary Spit Lamb

sprigs rosemary
2.25–3.2kg/5–7 lb leg of lamb,
   boned and rolled
salt and pepper
100g/4 oz butter, melted

Put the rosemary on the outside of the lamb and tie the roll securely. Rub with salt and pepper. Secure the lamb on the spit, brush with melted butter and cook over medium coals for 2–3 hours, basting with more butter during cooking. A meat thermometer should read 65°–70°C/150°–160°F.

Remove the lamb from the spit, place on a board and slice thinly.

Pleated Pork Ribs

2.7–3.6kg/6–8 lb pork spare ribs

SAUCE
60ml/4 tablespoons oil
4 onions, chopped
400g/14 oz canned chopped
   tomatoes
50g/2 oz Demerara sugar
65ml/2½ fl oz vinegar
150ml/¼ pint orange juice
salt and pepper

Make the sauce first. Heat the oil in a saucepan, add the chopped onions and fry for 3–4 minutes. Add the other sauce ingredients, and simmer gently for 10 minutes.

Sprinkle the spare ribs with salt and pepper and pleat the ribs on to the spit, putting the spit through the fleshy part after every fourth or fifth rib. Brush well with the sauce. Arrange the hot coals either at the back of the fire bowl or in two rows, with the drip pan beneath the meat. Allow the ribs to rotate over low coals for 1–1½ hours, brushing them with more sauce every 30 minutes.

Add a few twigs of dampened apple wood during the last 30 minutes of cooking.

VEGETABLES

Most vegetables can be prepared well in advance. Full use can then be made of the barbecue by cooking the vegetables on the grill or wrapping them in foil and cooking them directly in the coals. All can be kept very simple but a sauce or savoury topping adds extra flavour.

Saucy Onions

16 medium-sized onions
salt and pepper
soy sauce

Put the onions in pairs on to a square of heavy duty foil (or a double thickness of standard foil). Season with salt and pepper and a few drops of soy sauce. Bring the edges of the foil together to make a bundle, place amongst the hot coals and cook for 30–35 minutes.

Barbecued Corn-on-the-cob

Look for bright-green, snug husks (this shows the freshness) and the dark brown silk at the husk end – a sign of well-filled kernels.

Cook fresh corn as soon as possible after buying, or store in a refrigerator to preserve tenderness and sweet flavour.

To Cook

Serve one corn cob per person. Pull back the husks from the corn and remove the silk. Replace the husks and tie in place. Cook the corn in boiling salted water for 3–4 minutes, then drain. Cook on the barbecue grill over hot coals for 12–15 minutes, turning frequently. Remove the husks and serve the corn with butter and salt.

VARIATIONS

1) After boiling, the corn can be roasted in the coals for 10–12 minutes and then served as above.
2) Pull back the husks and remove the silk. Brush the corn with melted butter and sprinkle with salt and pepper. Pull the husks back over the corn again. Put each corn on a piece of foil, bring the sides of the foil together, twisting the ends to seal. Place the parcels on the grill and cook over hot coals for 20–30 minutes, turning each parcel once during cooking. A crushed clove of garlic can be added to the melted butter, before brushing on the corn.
3) Pull back the husks and remove the silk. Pour a barbecue sauce (pages 29–32) over the corn, pull back the husks and cook as above.

Courgette Boats

25g/1 oz butter
8 tomatoes, skinned, de-seeded and chopped
2 large onions, chopped
salt and pepper
2 cloves garlic, crushed
2.5ml/½ teaspoon oregano
8 large courgettes

Melt the butter in a frying pan, add the tomatoes and onions and fry for 4–5 minutes. Stir in the salt, pepper, garlic and oregano. Cut the courgettes in half lengthways. Sandwich two halves of courgette together again with some of the tomato mixture. Secure in two places with small pieces of cocktail stick. Wrap each courgette in a piece of foil and place on the grill. Cook over medium coals for 20–30 minutes.

Jacket Potatoes

8 large potatoes
50g/2 oz butter
salt
grated cheese
soured cream
chives **or** chopped parsley

Prick the potatoes all over, rub with butter and sprinkle with salt. Place each one on a square of double thickness foil. Bring the ends of the foil together in the centre and fold over two or three times. Turn the sides of the foil over twice and fold the ends underneath to make a sealed parcel. Push the parcels into the coals and cook for 50–60 minutes, turning once or twice during cooking. Pierce the foil with a fork to test that the potato is cooked. Open the parcel and cut a cross on the top of the potato.

Serve topped with butter, grated cheese, soured cream and chives or chopped parsley.

Golden Potatoes

50g/2 oz butter
50g/2 oz sugar
900g/2 lb cooked small new
   potatoes
salt

Melt the butter in a frying pan, stir in the sugar, and cook until the sugar has browned, stirring all the time. Add the potatoes and toss them until golden-brown. Sprinkle with salt before serving.

Potato Thins

8 large potatoes
2.5ml/½ teaspoon garlic salt
2.5ml/½ teaspoon celery salt
ground black pepper
30ml/2 tablespoons grated
   Parmesan cheese
225g/8 oz butter

Peel the potatoes and cut into thin chips. Mix together the seasonings and cheese. Divide the potato chips on to eight squares of foil, dot each with butter and sprinkle with the seasoning. Bring the edges of the foil together to make a bundle. Allow plenty of room for expansion of steam in each bundle. Cook the bundles on the grill over medium coals for 25–30 minutes or until the potatoes are tender when tested with a skewer. Turn the bundles several times during cooking.

Spicy Whole Tomatoes

50g/2 oz butter
50g/2 oz onion, chopped
50g/2 oz Demerara sugar
8 whole cloves
2 bay leaves
2 cinnamon sticks
5ml/1 teaspoon salt
ground black pepper
8 large tomatoes
soured cream
chopped parsley
paprika

Melt the butter in a small saucepan, add the onion and fry for 3–4 minutes. Add the sugar, cloves, bay leaves, cinnamon sticks, salt and pepper and cook for a further 2–3 minutes. Place each tomato on a double thickness of foil. Lift the foil round the tomato to form a cup. Cut a cross in the top of each tomato and spoon over some onion mixture. Gather the foil at the top to make a bundle. Place the bundles on the edge of the coals and cook for 30–35 minutes.

Carefully open the bundles and top each tomato with soured cream, chopped parsley and a dash of paprika.

Foiled Tomatoes

1 large onion
8 large firm tomatoes
oil
salt and pepper
5ml/1 teaspoon oregano

Cut the onion into eight thin slices. Cut the tomatoes in half crossways. Brush each half with oil and sprinkle with salt, pepper and a little oregano. Sandwich the tomato halves together again with a slice of onion in the middle, and secure with a cocktail stick. Place each tomato on a square of foil, and bring the corners of the foil together to form a bundle. Cook the bundles on the edge of the coals for 25–30 minutes until tender to the touch.

Stuffed Mushrooms

32 flat mushrooms
50g/2 oz butter
1 large onion, chopped
25g/1 oz grated cheese
50g/2 oz streaky bacon, chopped
50g/2 oz fresh white breadcrumbs
15ml/1 tablespoon chopped parsley
salt and pepper

Remove the mushrooms stalks and chop them finely. Melt the butter in a frying pan, add the mushroom stalks and onion, and fry for 3–4 minutes. Add the other ingredients, except the mushroom caps, and mix well. Stuff the mushroom caps with the mixture and put them on to squares of foil, four to a square. Bring the edges of the foil together to make a bundle, and cook on the grill over hot coals for 15–20 minutes.

Buttered Aubergines

4 aubergines
175g/6 oz butter
salt and pepper
ground nutmeg

Cut a thin slice from each end of each aubergine. Place each one on a piece of heavy duty foil (or a double thickness of standard foil), dot with butter and bring the edges together to make a bundle. Bake in the coals for 45–50 minutes or until tender. Carefully open the bundles. Slice the aubergines and serve sprinkled with salt, pepper and nutmeg and the melted butter.

Savoury Rice

50g/2 oz butter
100g/4oz onions, chopped
175g/6 oz smoked sausage
175g/6 oz long-grain rice, cooked
100g/4 oz cooked peas
2 tomatoes, de-seeded and
  chopped
butter
salt and pepper
2.5ml/½ teaspoon oregano

Melt the butter in a frying pan, add the onions and cook for 5 minutes. Cut the sausage into 1.25cm/½ inch slices, add to the onions and cook for 3–4 minutes. Stir in the rice and peas, then add the tomatoes with a knob of butter, the seasoning and oregano and heat for a further 5 minutes.

Note This mixture can be kept hot on the side of the grill.

SALADS

For crispness and goodness, a mixed green salad is the hardy perennial to serve with barbecued food. Try also, however, to have a good contrast in colour and texture so that the whole meal is attractive and appetizing. Most salad foods can be prepared well in advance but the dressing should be added just before serving.

Bean Sprout Salad

350g/12 oz fresh bean sprouts
100g/4 oz onion, chopped
2.5ml/½ teaspoon dried tarragon
5ml/1 teaspoon dry mustard
10ml/2 teaspoons Demerara sugar
150ml/¼ pint oil
30ml/2 tablespoons wine vinegar
chopped parsley

Put the bean sprouts into a bowl and stir in the onion. Mix together the other ingredients and pour them over the bean sprouts. Toss well and serve.

Hot Potato Salad

45ml/3 tablespoons wine vinegar
900g/2 lb small cooked new
  potatoes
12 spring onions, chopped
25g/1 oz chopped parsley
150ml/¼ pint oil
salt and pepper
150ml/¼ pint natural yogurt
paprika

Heat the vinegar in a saucepan, add the potatoes, onions, parsley, oil, salt and pepper, and simmer for 3–4 minutes. Fold in the yogurt, turn into a serving dish and sprinkle with paprika.

Note The salad can be kept hot in the saucepan on the side of the grill.

Spanish Salad

1 lettuce
8 tomatoes, skinned, de-seeded and
  chopped
100g/4 oz canned anchovy fillets,
  drained
225g/8 oz peeled prawns
16 Spanish stuffed olives, halved

DRESSING
150ml/¼ pint oil
60ml/4 tablespoons lemon juice
salt and pepper
1.25ml/¼ teaspoon dry mustard
1.25ml/¼ teaspoon sugar

GARNISH
4 hard-boiled eggs, sliced

Tear the lettuce into pieces and place in a salad bowl. Add the tomatoes with the anchovies, prawns and olives.
  Put the oil, lemon juice, salt, pepper, mustard and sugar into a screw-topped jar, cover and shake well.
  Pour the dressing over the salad and toss well. Garnish with the sliced hard-boiled eggs.

Sour Rice Salad

225g/8 oz long-grain rice, freshly
  cooked
300ml/½ pint natural yogurt
chopped parsley

Put the cooked rice back in its saucepan, add the yogurt and parsley, and heat through gently.

Note Do not overheat as the mixture may curdle.

Spicy Rice Salad

175g/6 oz long-grain rice, cooked
2 tomatoes, chopped
1 red apple, cored and chopped
1 green pepper, chopped
200g/7 oz canned whole kernel
   sweetcorn, drained
100g/4 oz button mushrooms, sliced
50g/2 oz raisins
50g/2 oz chopped walnuts
30ml/2 tablespoons French dressing
2.5ml/$\frac{1}{2}$ teaspoon ground nutmeg
salt and pepper

GARNISH
watercress

Serves 8–12

Put the rice in a bowl, add the other ingredients, and mix together well. Press the mixture into a 20cm/8 inch ring mould, and chill for 30 minutes in a refrigerator. Turn out on to a flat serving plate and fill the centre with watercress.

Note If no ring mould is available, pile the mixture into a salad bowl.

Chicory and Orange Salad

6 heads chicory
2 oranges, peeled
45ml/3 tablespoons French dressing

Cut the chicory into chunks. Cut the oranges into thin rounds, then mix together with the chicory and French dressing, and toss lightly.

Minted Cucumber and Celery Salad

1 medium-sized cucumber
100g/4 oz celery
10ml/2 teaspoons chopped mint
salt and pepper
juice of $\frac{1}{2}$ lemon
150ml/$\frac{1}{4}$ pint soured cream
chopped parsley

Thinly slice the cucumber and chop the celery. Mix together with the other ingredients and chill before serving.

Chicory and Orange Salad, Spicy Rice Salad **and** *Minted Cucumber and Celery Salad*

Tomato and Fennel Salad

450g/1 lb tomatoes
2 medium-sized roots fennel

DRESSING
60ml/4 tablespoons oil
30ml/2 tablespoons wine vinegar
salt and ground black pepper
5ml/1 teaspoon sugar
2.5ml/½ teaspoon dry mustard

Cut the tomatoes into quarters. Cut across the fennel root into thin rings and mix with the tomatoes. Put the dressing ingredients into a screw-topped jar, cover and shake well.

Pour the dressing over the salad just before serving.

Piquant Endive Salad

2 heads endive
1 bunch of watercress
225g/8 oz button mushrooms
juice of 1 lemon
salt and pepper
Piquant Dressing (page 32)

Toss together the endive and watercress. Slice the mushrooms thinly, sprinkle with lemon juice, salt and pepper, then toss lightly with the endive and mushrooms and the Piquant Dressing.

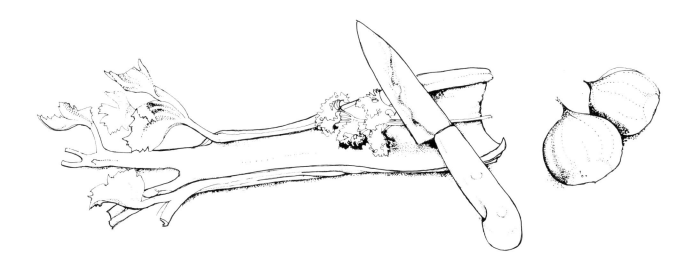

FRUIT AND DESSERTS

Fruit cooked on a barbecue has a most delicious flavour and contrasts well with the savoury foods enjoyed beforehand.

As an alternative, or in addition, serve a mouthwatering creamy concoction or a bowl of chilled fruit salad to round off the afternoon or evening.

Fruit Kebabs

orange segments
black and white grapes
pineapple pieces
apricot halves
bananas
cherries
pears
apples
butter, melted

Brush the fruit with melted butter and cook on the grill over medium coals for 8–10 minutes, turning several times during cooking.

VARIATION
For a different flavour, brush the fruit with a blend of melted butter, Demerara sugar and ground cinnamon.

Spiced Apples (page 92), Fruit Kebabs **and**, *in the background, Orange Cheesecake (page 93)* **and** *Bramble Syllabub (page 92)*

Spiced Apples

8 large cooking apples, cored
225g/8 oz mincemeat
100g/4 oz butter
5ml/1 teaspoon ground cloves
150ml/¼ pint natural yogurt

Make a slit round the centre of each apple to score the skin, then place each one on a square of double thickness foil. Fill the cavity with mincemeat, dot with butter, and sprinkle with ground cloves. Wrap the foil round the apples to make a bundle. Cook on the grill over hot coals for 30–40 minutes.

Serve the apples topped with yogurt.

Jamaican Grapefruit

4 grapefruit
60ml/4 tablespoons rum
60ml/4 tablespoons Demerara
  sugar
8 maraschino cherries

Cut the grapefruit in half and place each half on a double thickness of foil. Bring the edges up round the fruit, pour over the rum and sprinkle with sugar. Place a cherry in the centre of each fruit and twist the edges of the foil together to make a bundle. Put the bundles on the grill and heat over hot coals for 10–15 minutes.

Bramble Syllabub

450g/1 lb blackberries
30ml/2 tablespoons sugar
3 egg whites
300ml/½ pint double cream
175g/6 oz caster sugar
finely grated rind and juice of 2
  lemons
150ml/¼ pint dry white wine

Put the fruit with the sugar into a saucepan, reserving eight blackberries for decoration. Cook gently until the fruit is just soft. Leave to cool, then spoon into eight tall glasses.

Whisk the egg whites until stiff. Whip the cream until stiff, then fold into the egg whites with the caster sugar, lemon rind and juice and the wine.

Pile the mixture into the glasses and top each with a reserved berry.

Melon Party Bowl

½ watermelon
caster sugar
60ml/4 tablespoons sherry

Scoop out the flesh from the melon and put to one side. Cut a serrated edge to form a decorative shell. Dice the flesh or form into balls with a melon ball cutter. Put into a bowl with the sugar, and toss lightly until the sugar dissolves. Add the sherry and toss again. Pile into the melon shell and chill well before serving.

VARIATION
Cubes of other fresh fruit can be mixed with the watermelon to provide colour contrast.

Gingered Pears

1 litre/1¾ pints water
225g/8 oz sugar
12 ripe pears, peeled, quartered
  and cored
75g/3 oz preserved ginger,
  chopped
30ml/2 tablespoons ginger syrup

Put the water and sugar in a saucepan and heat to dissolve the sugar. Add the pears, ginger and syrup. Cover and simmer for 5–10 minutes until the pears are just tender. Carefully turn into a serving dish and leave to cool.
  Serve with whipped cream.

Orange Cheesecake

12 digestive biscuits
25g/1 oz cocoa powder
25g/1 oz caster sugar
70g/2½ oz butter, melted
450g/1 lb cream cheese
100g/4 oz icing sugar
275g/10 oz canned mandarin
  oranges
150ml/¼ pint double cream
orange rind, softened in boiling
  water

Crush the biscuits, then add the cocoa powder and sugar. Stir in the melted butter and press into the bottom of a foil lined 20cm/8 inch sponge tin. Chill in a refrigerator for 1–2 hours.
  Beat together the cheese and icing sugar until smooth. Drain the juice from the mandarin oranges and beat 30ml/ 2 tablespoons of the juice into the cheese mixture. Whip the cream until stiff and stir into the mixture. Pour into the prepared biscuit base and chill for 1–2 hours until set.
  To serve, lift the cheesecake out of the tin and carefully remove the foil. Place the cake on a serving dish and decorate with the mandarin oranges and orange rind.

BREAD

Hot Savoury Bread

1 long French loaf
100g/4 oz butter

FLAVOURINGS
5ml/1 teaspoon each chopped
 parsley and chives
 or
 2.5ml/½ teaspoon curry powder
 or
 2 cloves garlic, crushed
 or
2.5ml/½ teaspoon mixed herbs

Cut the French loaf diagonally into slices about 2.5cm/1 inch thick, but do not cut through the bottom crust. Cream the butter and flavourings, and use to spread the cut surfaces of the bread. Wrap the bread in foil and put on the grill or at the side of the coals to heat through for about 10 minutes, turning frequently.

Pitta Bread

This makes a very convenient 'pocket' or envelope in which to serve kebabs or burgers with a salad.

To use, heat in the oven or wrap in foil and heat on the grill of the barbecue. As it heats, the bread puffs up. Make a slit along the long side and use as required.

Cheese and Onion Round

1 round stoneground loaf
    (450–675g/1–1½ lb approx)
75g/3 oz butter
5ml/1 teaspoon prepared mustard
50g/2 oz grated Parmesan cheese
50g/2 oz onion, finely chopped
15ml/1 tablespoon chopped parsley
finely grated rind and juice of 1
    lemon

Serves 8–12

Cut the bread into 1.25cm/½ inch slices. Mix together the other ingredients and spread each slice of bread with the mixture. Put the loaf together again, cut in half through the centre and put on to a piece of foil. Gather the edges of the foil together to make a parcel and heat on the grill or at the side of the coals for about 20 minutes, turning frequently.

INDEX